By-Way Biking on the North York Moors

Roy Coleman

Published by Sigma Leisure – an imprint of
Sigma Press, 1 South Oak Lane, Wilmslow, Cheshire SK9 6AR, England.

British Library Cataloguing in Publication Data
A CIP record for this book is available from the British Library.

ISBN: 1-85058-714-0

Typesetting and Design by: Sigma Press, Wilmslow, Cheshire.

Cover design: MFP Design & Print; photograph – Spaunton Moor, above Rosedale *(Roy Coleman)*

Photographs and illustrations: Roy Coleman

Printed by: MFP Design & Print

Disclaimer: the information in this book is given in good faith and is believed to be correct at the time of publication. No responsibility is accepted by either the author or publisher for errors or omissions, or for any loss or injury howsoever caused. Only you can judge your own fitness, competence and experience.

Acknowledgements

It is only due to the help of a number of good friends that this book was completed at all. I would therefore like to take this opportunity to thank the following people:

Mr Winn Darley for allowing the use of the tracks from Rosedale Chimney Bank to Ana Cross and down towards Lastingham.

Viscount Ingleby for allowing the use of the tracks from Rasedale Mill and Barkers Ridge.

Mr Simon Forster for allowing the use of the Toll Road from Grosmont to Egton Bridge.

Ann and Irene for the typing.

Carl at the North York Moors National Park for vetting the routes.

Dan, Tom, Rollo, Charles, Gary and Andrew for the company when testing and documenting the routes.

Dan "the body" Spicer for his modeling expertise on the front cover. Did you notice all the designer clothing? – Dorothy Perkins!

Liz and Anna for plodding through all the text, lucking for spelin miscakes and grammar checking of whot I wrote.

Last but not least I would like to thank Liz for all the support throughout the project, "encouraging" me to go out in the snow and rain when I could have stayed home in front of a blazing fire. And for not resorting to violence when we are on a family day out and all I do is comment on the quality of the bridle paths. Without her encouragement this book would still be only an idea.

Contents

Introduction

Route Locations

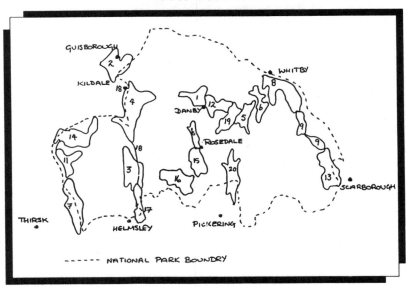

Route Summaries

Introduction

This guide has been written to present routes in a manner that is both easy and enjoyable to follow. Each route has been documented in two different ways so that you can follow direction diagrams by using a cycle computer in conjunction with the "Tulip Diagrams", or from the detailed written descriptions. Neither GPS nor AutoRoute® are required.

The routes are not meant to be an ordeal, they are to be enjoyed! They are circular rides, most having either a tearoom or public house part-way round. The start point of each route is identified with a grid reference to allow you to plot it on the map and sort out your approach route. You should carry either the Ordnance Survey's **Touring Map & Guide** (1 inch to 1 mile) or the larger scale (2.5 inches to 1 mile) **Outdoor Leisure maps** (Sheets 26 and 27). These cover all of the routes.

Rights of Access

As mountain bikers, you will probably be aware that you cannot ride everywhere you would like to. The Ordnance Survey maps show many tracks, but this does not mean you can use them all. Many of these cross private land. Public rights of way shown as bridleways on these maps are open to cyclists but footpaths are not. Bridleways are, however, not always easy to find as they may cross open moor on thick heather, or go through woods where there is no way through the thick undergrowth. Do not despair! Along with the passable bridleways there are a number of tracks shown on the map that are variously referred to as Green Lanes, Roads Used as Public Paths (RUPPs) or Byways Open to All Traffic (BOATs) are generally not marked as rights of way. This guide book uses a combination of these to give you a series of rides with the majority of the mileage being off-road.

There are also permissive bridleways. These are tracks and paths over private land where the landowner has given permission for these to be used – you have no right of way over them and permission can be withdrawn at any time. There is also a maze of tracks in the Forestry Commission plantations but there is only limited access to these and, in order to ride many of them, a permit is required from the Forestry Commission. Much effort has gone into making sure that all routes are on legal rights of way or have the express permission of the landowners – however, rights of access change from time to time as do the positioning of bridleways. Do not take this guide as a Rights of Access document.

The North York Moors National Park

The North York Moors National Park must be the best place for mountain biking in the UK, with very little of the area being un-rideable. The National Park is situated about half way up the length of the country, close to the market towns of Thirsk and Guisborough, and the seaside towns of Whitby and Scarborough. The area offers a rich network of bridleways and Green Lanes and boasts many picturesque moorland villages with steam trains, craft shops, rivers and – important for cy-clists – tearooms and pubs.

By Car

If you are travelling by car, the best way to get here is on the A1. Then, from either the north or the south, take the A168 towards Thirsk. From Thirsk you have a choice of roads depending upon which routes you in-tend to tackle first.

By Train

The nearest mainline station is Darlington. From Darlington take the lo-cal train to Middlesbrough, and change for the Whitby train that takes you through the picturesque Esk valley, travelling through the heart of the national park.

By Bike

If you are travelling to the area by bike – you must be *very* keen, so I'm not going to tell you how to get here at all.

Touring

If you are touring the area by bike, Castleton (Moorlands Hotel – 01287 660206) and Danby (Duke of Wellington – 01287 660351) are on the Middlesborough to Whitby train route and make good bases for many of the routes. Other villages on the train route are Kildale, Lealholm and Glaisdale; these make good starting points and have bed and breakfast acommodation available. For those who prefer to spend their nights under canvas, there are good campsites at Rosedale Abbey (01751 417272) and Spiers House in Cropton Forest (01751 417591).

There is an excellent, low-cost "Moors Bus" that stops at many villages.

Tourist Information Centres

Information on local accommodation and public transport is available from TICs:

Danby (Moors Centre): 01287 660654

Great Ayton: 01642 722835

Whitby: 01947 602124

Tearooms

Almost all of the routes pass tearooms and telephone numbers are provided so that you can enquire about opening times.

Route	Tearoom	Telephone
1.	Stonehouse Bakery, Danby	01287 660006
2.	Glebe Cottage Tearoom, Kildale	01642 724470
4.	Glebe Cottage Tearoom, Kildale	01642 724470
5.	Beggars Bridge Tearooms, Glaisdale station	
6.	Hazelwood Tearoom, Grosmont	01947 895292
7.	Sutton Bank Visitor Centre	01845 597426
8.	Beacon Farm Tearoom	01947 605212
9.	Smugglers Rock Tearoom, Ravenscar	01723 870044
10.	Shepherds Hall Tearoom, Lealholm	01947 897361
11.	Chequers, above Osmotherly	01609 883291
12.	Stonehouse Bakery, Danby	01287 660006
13.	Yew Tree Café, Scalby	01723 367989
14.	Lord Stone Café, Carlton	01642 778227
15.	Bakery Tearoom, Rosedale	
16.	The Forge Tearoom, Hutton-le-Hole	01751 417444
17.	Thomas the Baker, Kirkbymoorside	01751 432641
18.	Glebe Cottage Tearoom, Kildale	01642 724470
19.	Shepherds Hall Tearoom, Lealholm	01947 897361
20.	Farworth Tea Garden (Mrs Eddon)	01751 477244

Grid References

An Ordinance Survey map is divided into squares (grid squares). Each of these is identified by a series of vertical and horizontal grid lines. The distance between each of these is 1 kilometre (see Figure 1).

The scale of the particular map will affect the amount of detail visible. For example the "Outdoor Leisure" series of maps are scaled at 4 cm = 1 km, whereas the "Landranger" series has a scale of 2 cm = 1 km. However, a grid square on either map always represents an area of 1 square kilometre. For a better accuracy than 1km we can imagine the distance between each grid line being divided into 10 more grid lines – see Figure 2. This enables us to locate positions to within 100 metres.

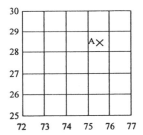

Figure 1: point A is located between vertical lines 75 and 76; divide the square into 10 giving a horizontal reference of 756

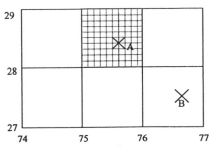

Figure 2: the vertical grid lines are also sub-divided into 10 giving point A a vertical grid reference of 284. As the horizontal reference is always given before the vertical, the full grid reference for point A is 756284. Point B is at grid reference 766275

Tulip Diagrams

Tulip diagrams are more commonly used in motor rallying, but are just as useful for mountain biking. They are used to represent a point on a route – for example, the layout of a junction or the route through a farm-yard – together with the direction of travel. They also show the distance to ride from the previous Tulip diagram.

Total	Split	Description	Tulip Diag
5.91	0.73	Past farm on left, then through gate and passing a dry stone wall on your left.	

The example shown above has four headings, the function of each is as follows:

Total: When the total mileage on your cycle computer shows this distance you should be at, or near the landmark indicated by the tulip diagram.

Split: This is the distance between the previous Tulip diagram landmark and this one.

Description: This is a description of the landmark that you are passing together with any useful information.

Tulip Diag: This diagram shows that you pass a farm on your left prior to passing through a gate. You then go straight ahead with a dry stone wall on your left. The symbols used for the diagrams should be self explanatory.

The route is made up of a series of these Tulip diagrams together with grid references for start and finish points.

Safety First

Headgear

Before you think of setting out, always be sure to wear your helmet. If you are new to mountain biking, and not sure which type of helmet to buy, find a good mountain bike shop and ask! The cheapest is not always the best buy – neither is the most expensive. The important thing is that the helmet fits correctly. Try it on; if the shop won't let you, go to a different shop. Check that it has the British Standard kite mark on it. Please wear it.

Information

Always make sure that someone knows your route and what time you will be back. Even though you may only be out for an hour or two, and a few hundred metres from a road, you can still have a serious accident. If you've had an accident and can't move, someone with your route will know where to look for you.

Ride in Groups

Ride with a few friends – if one of you has an accident, others can go for help. If one of your party needs to go for assistance, it is important that they don't rush and have an accident themselves, one is more than enough. If you do ride alone take some means of identification with you, then if you are ill or take a fall at least whoever finds you will know who to contact, or where to drop the body off!

The ideal minimum is four persons on an excursion. If one person is injured, two people can go for help leaving one with the casualty. It's not a good idea for one person to go for help on his own. Before anyone goes for help, write down your position, either as a grid reference or take note of the nearest farms or landmarks.

Mobile phones are a great method of getting help, however, be aware that the coverage on the moors is patchy at best with little or no coverage in the low valleys.

First Aid Kit

Always carry a first aid kit with you. You may think "it won't happen to me" – I hope it doesn't, but if it does, be prepared. The minimum to carry with you is:

🚲 A small bandage

🚲 Sterile gauze

🚲 A tube of Savlon or similar antiseptic cream

🚲 Plasters

It's worth keeping a copy of *First Aid on Mountains* with you. It is written by Steve Bollen and published by the British Mountaineering Council. You can order this from your local bookshop.

Mountain Rescue

If you have the misfortune to need help, either for yourself or a companion, Cleveland Search and Rescue team can be called out by dialling 999 and asking for Search and Rescue.

The Kit

Before you undertake an adventure, you must at least have a bike. However I suggest you don't set off on any ride without at least some other equipment. The checklist below is a good guide to some of the more important items you should take.

Essential

🚲 **Safety helmet**

🚲 **Waterproof clothing**

🚲 **Map** and **compass**

🚲 **First Aid Kit** – and book.

🚲 **Food** and **drink**

🚲 **Pump** and spare **inner tube**

- **Tyre levers** – can you change an inner tube on the moors? If the answer is not a resounding "yes", it's worth having a practice at home

- **Route plan** – leave it with somebody back at base, together with your estimated time of return

- **Whistle** – to attract attention

- **Lights** – if you may be out after dark

- **Bright coloured clothing** – so you can be seen

- **A watch** – so you can time your trip to get off the moor before it gets dark

- **Change** for the phone

Useful

- **Tool kit** – it's worth getting one of the many "multitools" available, it will do 90% of repairs.

- **Tools** – if you are going to buy some, it's worth getting good ones. Go to your local mountain bike shop and have a word with the mechanic for his advice on what to buy

- **Chain splitter** – useful if your chain breaks miles from anywhere, I've used mine twice on the moor and avoided a five-mile walk back to the car.

- **Mobile phone** – will have patchy coverage, but useful if you can hop to the top of hills where you get a good signal.

- **A compass** – if you get lost in fog, you will be able to take a bearing and get safely off the moors.

General

- Keep your bike in **good condition**, if it is well maintained it is less likely to cause you any problems.

- Wear **several layers** of thinner clothes rather than one thick garment, it's warmer and helps to keep out the wind.

- Apply **sun screen** in summer: if you are riding in T-shirt and shorts it doesn't take long to get burnt.

Route 1

The Commondale Round

Total Distance: 10.00 miles   **Offroad:** 66%

Start/Finish: Grid reference 663105 (Commondale)

This route starts at the Cleveland Inn public house in Commondale. If you are arriving by car, the best parking seems to be on the hill on the road out to Kildale. Having parked your car, packed your sandwiches and had six pints of lager in the pub you should be ready to set out.

With the pub on your right and the small village green on your left, follow the level tarmac road past the fishing lakes on your right. After about a quarter of a mile the road bends to the left and a bridleway is signposted left past a farmhouse – Foul Green (that's the name of the place – not the colour of the house). Follow this track, passing the footpath on the right to Commondale railway station. Go through a gate and left around the front of a house, stay on the wide main bridleway through a gate by a dry stone wall, passing a small group of trees.

As you look ahead you can see the bridleway you are riding as it follows the side of the valley above the course of the Middlesbrough to Whitby railway.

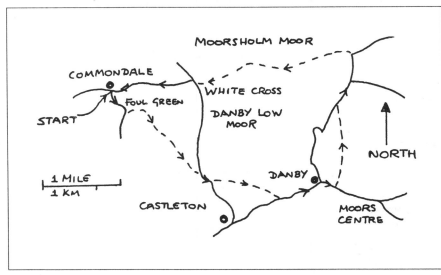

After about a third of a mile the track goes through a small wood and a few houses on your right. Three-quarters of a mile further on you pass Box Hall also on your right. Continue up the hill on gravel track until it joins the Lockwood Beck to Castleton road. Turn right at this junction and head downhill towards Castleton. About 200 metres down this hill on the left, there is a wooden signpost with carved fish on it pointing "Danby 2 miles".

Unless you wish to continue on into Castleton to visit the tearooms in the village at the top of the hill or the ice-cream van that is often parked by the river bridge in the valley bottom, turn left onto this signed track. (If you are starting the route from Castleton bridge, set off up the hill under the railway bridge until you see the "Fish & Danby 2 miles" sign on your right about 250 metres after the railway.)

Follow the Danby signed path above the tennis court and past a few houses on your right. From this vantage point half way up the valley side you can look across to Castleton village on the opposite hilltop and down onto the cricket pitch and River Esk. After about quarter of a mile the bridleway splits in two directions, follow the track to your right following a dry stone wall.

Keeping on the main track, go through a wooded area (Danby Park) and then out onto open moorland. After about 350 metres there is a track on the left that joins the bridleway that you are riding, that track is part of the Pannierman's Causeway that eventually leads to Scalling Dam reservoir. Keep right at this point continuing down to the junction with the tarmac road. Turn left onto the road and follow it into Danby village where you will see the Duke Of Wellington pub head of you.

Go straight ahead at the cross-roads passing the pub, shop and tearoom (set back off the road) and continue up the hill for about 250 metres until you see a bridleway sign on the left-hand side of the road. Turn left after the terrace of houses onto a tarmac track, and follow this as it doubles back on itself and heads uphill. The tarmac finishes after about 30 metres and turns into a grassy track. The track forks here; take the left-hand track that passes the entrance drive to a house. You will soon arrive at two gates side by side; go through the left-hand gate.

Ignoring the two tracks on your left, go straight ahead on a stony track up-hill and over the ridge. Keep going in this direction until you come to the corner of a dry stone wall, follow the track with the wall to your right until you come to a gate in the wall (after about 30 metres).

Do not follow the path along by the wall, but take the path at 90° on your left that looks as though you have come out of the gate and gone straight ahead (see the sketch on the route card marked 4.36 miles). This path then bends to

The Old Post Office Tearoom

the right and goes out over the open moor – this path is called The Lord's Turnpike.

Stay on this easy to follow track for about three-quarters of a mile until it joins the tarmac road and turn right onto the road and cross Black Beck bridge. Follow this road straight ahead for 1 mile until the main road turns right at a series of black and white chevrons. Turn left onto a wide track across Gerrick Moor and Tomgate Moor for two and a quarter miles until you again meet a tarmac road at White Cross. (Note that the track may become boggy in the middle section following very wet weather). Cross the Lockwood Beck to Castleton road and proceed straight ahead along the tarmac road downhill for one and a quarter miles back to the start in Commondale.

ROUTE1		LOCATION - COMMONDALE AND DANBY ROUND	DISTANCE	
66% OFFROAD		DIFFICULTY - EASY	9.55 MILES	

SPLIT DISTANCE	TOTAL DISTANCE	DESCRIPTION BETWEEN POINTS	DIAGRAM OF LOCATION
0	0	Start from Cleveland Inn public house in Commondale (Grid Ref. 663105) leave towards Westerdale with pub on right and village green on left. Fishing lakes on right	
0.25	0.25	Bear left onto a signed bridleway in front of farmhouse	
0.08	0.33	Go though gate and around house on left. Track turns left and then right after the house	
0.25	0.58	Straight ahead through gate, track follows valley side overlooking the railway track	
0.24	0.82	Stay on track through a small group of trees and pass some houses on your right	
0.75	1.57	Pass a house on your right and carry on up a gravel track uphill	
0.43	2	Bridleway joins main Lockwood Beck to Castleton road Go straight ahead downhill towards Castleton	
0.15	2.15	As you go downhill towards Castleton look for a wooden sign on your left with a fish carved on it and take this track	
		NOTE If you pass the tennis court on your left you have gone too far down the hill	
0.21	2.36	Follow the track around the dry stone wall, do not take the track that goes left and uphill.	
		Go through a small wood and out onto open moorland	
0.97	3.33	Follow the track right and downhill towards the Tarmac road	

ROUTE1		LOCATION - COMMONDALE AND DANBY ROUND	DISTANCE
66% OFFROAD		DIFFICULTY - EASY	9.55 MILES
SPLIT DISTANCE	TOTAL DISTANCE	DESCRIPTION BETWEEN POINTS	DIAGRAM OF LOCATION
0.11	3.44	Join the road by turning left towards Danby	
0.49	3.93	Straight over at the crossroads. Stop at the Duke of Wellington for a pint , the shop next door for an ice-cream or the tea room 30 meters up the road for a pot of tea	PUB
0.15	4.08	Turn left after a row of houses onto a tarmac track as it doubles back on itself and then turns into a grassy surface. Track forks after 30 metres, take left hand track	HOUSE
0.13	4.21	Two gates side by side, take the right hand gate and follow the track uphill straight ahead.	
0.15	4.36	Follow the track to a stone wall and follow with the wall on your right until you come to a gate in the wall	GATE
		Follow the track opposite the gate as it turns 90 degrees right and onto the moor, do not follow the center track.	WALL
0.72	5.08	The track you have just come across is called the Lords Turnpike. Turn right onto Tarmac road and over the bridge	
0.95	6.03	As the road turns right, turn left onto a wide stony track	
2.3	8.33	Stay on this sometimes rough track for 2.3 miles until you come to the junction at White Cross	
1.2	9.53	Cross the Lockwood Beck to Castleton road and go downhill on Tarmac for 1.2 miles back to the start	GREEN
		NOTE At Castleton you can go straight ahead past the Danby sign and carry on to the bottom of the hill over the bridge and up the other side into Castleton	
		where there are pubs and a tea room. In the summer there is normally an ice-cream van parked at the bridge at the bottom of the hill next to the river	

Route 2

Kildale, Roseberry and Hutton

Total Distance: 11.84 miles   **Off-road:** 74%

Start/Finish: Grid reference 607094 (Kildale)

This is a particularly good ride in July and August. The route starts at the tearooms in Kildale, where the home-made soup comes strongly recommended. Start from the tearoom near Kildale railway station. Park in the car park at the Kildale railway station and turn left out of the car park back towards Kildale. Once you come to the tearoom reset your trip computer to zero as the mileage readings start here.

Starting from the tearoom car park, leave through the opening onto the tarmac road and turn right.

Follow the road downhill and under the railway bridge, continue on through trees and over a cattle grid. After about 0.5 miles the road turns right around a building, stay on this tarmac road as it turns back left and up hill passing Bankside Farm on your left. This road continues uphill through Pale End Plantation and then drops down past Lonsdale Farm on your right and Oaktree Farm on your left. You have now ridden 1.43 miles from the start point. Where the road turns sharp left around the farm building, continue straight ahead through a gate and uphill on a rutted track into Lonsdale Plantation.

Stay on the main track uphill through the wood until you join with a tarmac road on the far side of the wood. Turn right along this road with Lonsdale plantation on your right for about 0.6 miles until you come to a green bridleway sign on your left (the "Private Road to Sleddale" sign does not apply to cycles), go left onto this track down hill, and across Sleddale beck. Follow this track until it turns right through a gate to the farm, do not go through this gate but instead go ahead onto a rougher track and fork left as it goes uphill. This track continues for 1.17 miles across the open Gisborough Moor as it heads towards the trees of Highcliff Wood.

Just before you reach the wood, the track forks into three. Take the left of these tracks as it continues to a wide gate in the dry stone wall. If you find yourself at the small gate at the corner of the wood, you need to turn left and with the wall on your right continue for about 30 metres until you come to the wide gate. Go through this gate following the track ahead through two further wide gates until you come to a small gate in the wall in front of the trees. Go through this small gate onto a grassy path for about 75 metres, and where you join the main forest track turn right and follow it downhill. As you continue down this main track, you come to a clearing in the wood with a fence area on your left and gravel car park on your right.

Continue on through this clearing and after about 200 metres you come to a junction — this junction is recognised by the prominent "hanging cliff" high up in the tree line on the left — turn right at this point going steeply downhill to a gate at the bottom. As you go through this gate continue through Hutton Village on tarmac road. After 0.5 miles, the road sweeps right with a terrace of houses set back about 100 metres on your right. Take the gate opposite the track to these houses. Follow the lower track on your left as it doubles back on itself and joins the path that is a short cut across the field. Go through the gate and into Hutton Lowcross Woods. Stay on this main track until the path splits after about half a mile, do not take the downhill path to the right but continue ahead. After another a quarter of a mile the track bends to the left and uphill, take the smaller grassy track straight ahead.

After about 200 metres on this path the wood on the right opens up to give

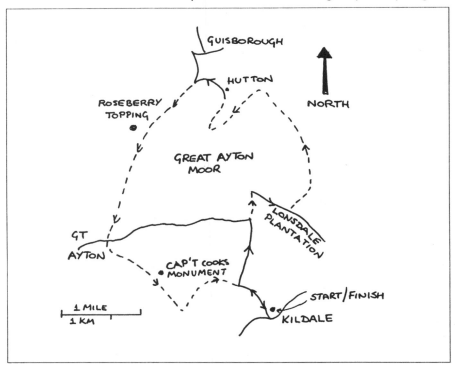

good views of Roseberry Topping and the surrounding River Tees area. Stay on this rough path through two gates until you are faced with the path splitting into three (just after the second gate), take the centre path slightly uphill as it passes to the left of Roseberry Topping. About 0.3 miles from this gate a track on your left goes steeply uphill towards the ridge – do not take this path but continue ahead with a wire fence on your left. Stay on this track as it goes through a gate and towards Airy Holme Farm. Follow the track left then right around the farmhouse and then down a tarmac road for 0.56 miles until you come to a crossroad junction with Dikes Lane.

Go straight ahead over the crossroads, the track soon thins out to a narrow stone path between hedges, then uphill through a group of trees and out onto open moorland. Pass through a gate following the path through Gorse bushes as it continues uphill for about 0.37 miles, stay on the main path as it enters Ayton Banks Wood. Soon after you exit the wood there is a wooden signpost showing a footpath to the right – keep straight ahead on the bridleway, passing the footpath, and then keep to the lower of the two tracks ahead – do not take the uphill track. Follow the narrow track though bracken until you come to a stone wall where the track forks just after the wall, keep to the left of the two tracks as it goes straight ahead into the wood. Soon this narrow path meets a wide forest track, turn left here onto the wide track and follow it for about 0.8 miles until you join a tarmac road (you may recognise this road as the one that you rode up when you first started the route). Turn right and follow the road back to the tearoom or car.

Roseberry Topping from Guisborough Woods

		LOCATION - KILDALE ROSEBERRY & HUTTON	DISTANCE
74% OFFROAD		DIFFICULTY - FAIRLY EASY - NO HARD CLIMBS	11.48 MILES
SPLIT DISTANCE	TOTAL DISTANCE	DESCRIPTION BETWEEN POINTS	DIAGRAM OF LOCATION
		Start from the tea-room in Kildale (Grid Ref 607094) Park the car at the station card park and ride back to the tea-room and zero your trip computer	
0	0	Leave the tea-room car park and turn right onto tarmac and slightly downhill	
0.15	0.15	Follow road downhill and over railway bridge	
0.37	0.52	Follow road around a 90 degree right hand corner near a building. Follow the road going left uphill through woods then downhill passing a farm on your right	
0.91	1.43	As road goes left around farm continue ahead through gate	
0.09	1.52	Uphill with wood on your right. Follow the main track into Lonsdale Plantation	
0.44	1.96	Stay on main track until it meets with a tarmac road at the edge of the woods. Turn right.	
0.57	2.53	Look for green bridleway sign on left and stone sign saying "Private road to Sledale". Turn left here - this sign does not apply to bikes	
0.64	3.17	Main track goes right through gate to farm, do not take this but go ahead and follow the track that forks left and uphill. Stay on this track onto open moor	
1.17	4.34	Just before the wood that track forks into 3, take the left hand fork and follow to a wide gate in a wall Go through the gate and ahead across field	
0.04	4.38	Through gate with stone wall on your right 30 metres away	
0.12	4.5	Go through another gate and cross field towards woods and a small gate	

ROUTE2		LOCATION - KILDALE ROSEBERRY & HUTTON	DISTANCE
74% OFFROAD		DIFFICULTY - FAIRLY EASY - NO HARD CLIMBS	11.48 MILES
SPLIT DISTANCE	TOTAL DISTANCE	DESCRIPTION BETWEEN POINTS	DIAGRAM OF LOCATION
0.14	4.64	Go through small gate and onto narrow grass track for 75 metres to meet wide track	
0.06	4.7	Left onto wide forest track	
0.09	4.79	Ignore track on right	
0.15	4.94	Ignore track on left, continue downhill on main track	
0.19	5.13	Through clearing in woods with fenced area on left and car parking on right	
0.15	5.28	Turn right steeply downhill on wide track	
0.23	5.51	Through gate and ahead on tarmac through Hutton Village	
0.58	6.09	Through small gate into field and follow track until it meets with a gate	
0.17	6.26	Through gate and into the wood	
0.51	6.77	Straight ahead ignoring track off on right then left	
0.23	7	As track bends left uphill, take smaller track straight ahead	
0.29	7.29	Through gate	

ROUTE2		LOCATION - KILDALE ROSEBERRY & HUTTON	DISTANCE
74% OFFROAD		DIFFICULTY - FAIRLY EASY - NO HARD CLIMBS	11.48 MILES
SPLIT DISTANCE	TOTAL DISTANCE	DESCRIPTION BETWEEN POINTS	DIAGRAM OF LOCATION
0.09	7.38	Through gate and follow path straight ahead uphill ignore tracks on left and right	
0.3	7.68	Ahead through gate ignoring steep path on left. Roseberry Topping on your right	
0.73	8.41	Through gate and follow track left then right around Airy Holme Farm	
0.56	8.97	Follow tarmac track downhill passing buildings to crossroads (Dikes Lane). Continue straight ahead staying on tarmac track	
0.17	9.14	Tarmac track turn into stone track between hedges	
0.28	9.42	Track narrows and goes through a group of trees then comes out onto open fields. Continue ahead uphill between gorse bushes	
0.37	9.79	Track passes path on right then through gate into woods	
0.34	10.13	Wooden sign points out bridleway and footpaths After sign the track forks, keep right here	
0.24	10.37	Good ride through though thick bracken in (July and August) to stone wall. Through gap in wall and straight ahead into wood	
0.16	10.55	Follow path through wood until it meets with wide track. Go left	
0.63	11.18	Follow track round to left	
0.14	11.32	Turn right where bridleway meets tarmac and follow road back to tea-room in Kildale 0.52 miles away	

Route 3

Farndale, Bransdale, Fadmoor and Gillamoor

Total Distance: 21.2 miles   **Offroad:** 57%

Start/Finish: Grid reference 673953 (Low Mill)

This route takes in part of Farndale, crosses over Rudland Rigg into Bransdale onto Kirk Dale, through Fadmoor and Gillamoor. It has three fairly steep, but not too long, climbs (out of Farndale, Bransdale and Kirk Dale), the remainder being less strenuous.

Car parking is at Low Mill — Grid Reference above, where there is a small car park with toilets.

Start by turning right out of the car park and uphill on tarmac, after about 0.25 miles you will see a sign pointing to the left marked "Bridleway to Rudland Rigg". Turn onto this bridleway towards a house (Horn End), and when you reach the house go straight ahead on a grassy track through a gate. Follow this track through another gate following a wire fence on your left, the track goes through more gates and past an old farm building on your left (High Barn), soon after passing this the building go through a gate and on towards another. Do not go through this gate but follow the Yellow and Blue waymark left and around the outside of the dry stone wall.

Go through a gate and over the wooden bridge that crosses the River Dove, follow the track as it heads uphill towards the ridge ahead. Keep left by the stone wall until you come to a gate in it, go through this gate and follow the path uphill (keeping to the right of the two trees ahead). The path curves to the right as it goes uphill and meets a small grass track. Go right as it continues uphill through bracken. Go through a gate with a waymark and follow the track as it gets steeper through the bracken, the track soon levels off and follows the side of the valley parallel with the ridge on a small path over heather. Start to go uphill past some grouse butts until you join a wide, stoned track on the top of the ridge. The wide track is Rudland Rigg, which runs south from the road at Baysdale (above Kildale) and joins a tarmac road about 2 miles north-west of Gillamoor. At this point, you have ridden 2.64 miles.

Turn right onto Rudland Rigg for about 0.5 miles until you come to cross-roads, then turn left onto another wide track. After about 0.4 miles you pass a track off on your left — keep straight ahead towards the radio mast you can see on the horizon (Bilsdale Mast). Go on through a gate and downhill into

Bransdale, turn right when you meet the tarmac road at Cow Sike Farm, then downhill until you come to a road junction signposted to Helmsley.

Follow the road round to the left and over a cattle grid (do not go ahead uphill towards Bransdale Lodge). After another 0.6 miles you come to another junction at a gate, do not turn left but go though the gate — signposted to Helmsley — and uphill on tarmac. Pass a track then a bridleway on your right and a small wood on your left as you continue up the incline. Pass another wider bridleway on your right as you come to the top of the bank.

Now follow the level, straight, tarmac road for 0.7 miles until it turns about 45 degrees to the right. With a small wood on your left follow the track straight-ahead (same direction that you've just come from), do not take the track that goes down towards the wood. This track that takes you over the small hill ahead (Lambfold Hill) has been used by off-road vehicles and is cut up quite badly in places. After about 1.35 miles along this track you come to a crossroads; go straight ahead for another 1.2 miles staying on the main track as it keeps to the left-hand side of the hill ahead (Birk Nab).

You come to a gate. Looking straight ahead, you can see the path that you are going to follow as it climbs steeply up Rollgate Bank. Go through the gate and up the steep hill ahead. At the top òf the hill go through another gate and follow the track ahead for 0.4 miles through a group of trees and through a further gate. You have now cycled 10.6 miles — about halfway through your ordeal.

Follow a wide track downhill past High Farm on your left, onto tarmac road and straight ahead passing Middle Farm (also on your left). About 0.25 miles after Middle farm you will see two wooden bridleway signs, one to the left and one to the right. Take the path to the left and follow down the edge of the field with the hedge on your right as it heads towards the wood. Pass through the gate into the wood, downhill into the valley and across the track in the bottom of the wood. Go straight ahead up the other side and out onto the road. Turn left onto the road then immediately right, going past the private road to Norton Tower. Follow the road ahead as it passes a turn off on the right to Pasture Cottage, after about 0.5 miles you come to a T-junction — turn right here and pass open fields for 1 mile until you come to a farm on your left. At this point you can see two bridleway signs close together, take the left-hand track towards the farm.

As you approach the farm keep to the right and through a gate onto a wide track, follow this as it doubles back behind the farm and through a gate into the wood. About 250 metres into the wood you will see a wide track on your right. About 50 metres after this track look for a bridleway sign on the right-hand side of the track. Take this small path as it goes downhill through nettles towards the river in the valley bottom (you are now in the bottom of Kirk Dale). Once the river is reached, you have to ford across it — the bridge along to your left is no right-of-way. Turn left on the far side of the river as the path follows a barbed wire fence uphill. After about 150 metres a field opens out ahead of you, look across this field in line with a row of spaced out trees towards the wood on the other side of the field. You will see a gate in the wire fence! Pass through this gate and follow the path around to the left as it fol-lows the wire fence, when it starts to bear right and climb uphill you pass a very steep track on your right. Soon after passing this track, you will see the path that you are following get steeper as it climbs a long straight incline.

After about 300 metres the incline meets a wider track. Turn left onto this track for another 350 metres until it emerges from the wood. Turn left onto this track (called Caldron Mill Road) for about 300 metres where it joins a tarmac road (called Green Lane), go right onto this road for about 600 metres and turn left at a T-junction signposted to Fadmoor. Continue until you reach another T-junction where you again turn left.

As you enter Fadmoor you may just want to stop for a pint or three at the pub on the left. When you decide to press on, turn right by the pub and follow the road for about 0.5 miles into Gillamoor where the Oak Tree pub may tempt you to make another stop. Follow the main road through Gillamoor passing a road off to the right and continue past the church and out of the village, the road goes downhill for over 0.5 miles to a junction signposted to Farndale. Turn left along the Farndale road and uphill for nearly a mile where you turn right onto a wide bridleway, this wide track follows downhill for over 0.5 miles, through a gate and into a farmyard (Park Farm). Keeping left of the farm pass through a gate then forward until you come to an open gate hole, do not go through here but turn left and follow the path, keeping the stone wall on your right. This easy to follow track continues alongside the wall through bracken until it comes to another gate, after this gate the track descends to Cross Farm, go straight ahead up a wide, stony track for about 200 metres where it joins a tarmac road. Turn right onto this road and follow it for 1.1 miles as it goes downhill back to the car park.

		LOCATION - BRANSDALE & FARNDALE	DISTANCE
58% OFFROAD		DIFFICULTY - MEDIUM WITH A FEW LONG CLIMBS	21.2 MILES
SPLIT DISTANCE	TOTAL DISTANCE	DESCRIPTION BETWEEN POINTS	DIAGRAM OF LOCATION
		Start from the car park at Low Mill in Farndale Grid Ref. 603953 Toilets available in car park	
0	0	Right out of car park and uphill	
0.25	0.25	Left onto bridleway signed Rudland Rigg	
0.32	0.57	Ahead through gate onto grassy track with a house on your left hand side	
0.19	0.76	Follow track by a wire fence as it goes through three gates	
0.26	1.02	Old farm buildings on left hand side	
0.06	1.08	Follow yellow & blue waymark sign through a gate and around the outside of a stone wall. Do not go through the second gate but keep left	
0.06	1.14	Through a gate then left over a small river bridge then ahead towards the ridge in front of you with the stone wall on your left until you come to a gate	
0.1	1.24	Go through gate and follow track uphill, keep to the right of two trees ahead	
0.13	1.37	Follow track as it turns right on a smaller grass track uphill through bracken	
0.07	1.44	Through gate and uphill following yellow and blue waymark sign. Track levels out and runs parallel with the ridge on a track through heather	
0.85	2.29	Track follows to the right of shooting butts	

SPLIT DISTANCE	TOTAL DISTANCE	DESCRIPTION BETWEEN POINTS	DIAGRAM OF LOCATION
		LOCATION - BRANSDALE & FARNDALE	DISTANCE
58% OFFROAD		DIFFICULTY - MEDIUM WITH A FEW LONG CLIMBS	21.2 MILES
0.35	2.64	Junction with Rudland Rigg, turn right onto wide track	
0.47	3.11	Turn left off Rudland Rigg onto a similar wide track	
0.43	3.54	Straight ahead towards Bilsdale radio mast ignore track on left	
0.35	3.89	Through gate and downhill into Bransdale	
0.39	4.28	Turn right when track meets tarmac road at Cow Sike farm	
0.46	4.74	Follow road to left over cattle grid, following the road signed to Helmsley Do not go ahead into Bransdale Lodge	
0.58	5.32	Through gate and uphill following signpost to Helmsley	
0.22	5.55	Track joins from right	
0.55	6.1	Wood on left	
0.46	6.56	Bridleway joins from right	
0.68	7.24	As road bends 45 degrees to right, go straight ahead on track. Do not take the left hand track that curves round towards the small wood. (Track may be rough)	
1.36	8.6	Ahead at crossroads as track goes uphill staying left of the hill ahead (Birk Nab)	

		LOCATION - BRANSDALE & FARNDALE	DISTANCE
58% OFFROAD		DIFFICULTY - MEDIUM WITH A FEW LONG CLIMBS	21.2 MILES
SPLIT DISTANCE	TOTAL DISTANCE	DESCRIPTION BETWEEN POINTS	DIAGRAM OF LOCATION
1.28	9.88	Through gate. - You can see Rollgate Bank ahead follow this track as it goes uphill	
0.73	10.61	Through gate at top of Rollgate Bank passing a group of trees	
0.37	10.98	Through gate then downhill passing High Farm Continue on tarmac road passing Middle Farm	
1.41	12.39	Turn off tarmac onto a bridleway (wooden signpost shows two tracks - turn left NOT right)	
0.16	12.55	Go into wood through gate and cross track in the bottom of the dip. Follow the track uphill.	
0.04	12.59	Onto tarmac going first left and then immediately right Do not use the private road to Nawton Tower	
0.18	12.77	Ignore the track on your right to Pasture Cottage	
0.51	13.28	Turn right at junction	
0.92	14.2	Turn left at wooden bridleway sign going through gate on the right just before the farm buildings Follow the wide track	
0.35	14.55	Through gate and into wood	
0.08	14.63	Look for wooden sign on right just after a track on your right. Follow signpost on small path into wood as it goes downhill to the left. Stay on track towards river	
0.22	14.85	Cross river & turn left following a barbed wire fence.	

		LOCATION - BRANSDALE & FARNDALE	DISTANCE
58% OFFROAD		DIFFICULTY - MEDIUM WITH A FEW LONG CLIMBS	21.2 MILES

SPLIT DISTANCE	TOTAL DISTANCE	DESCRIPTION BETWEEN POINTS	DIAGRAM OF LOCATION
		As track comes out into open field (about 150 meters) look across towards a gate by the wood opposite the gate is in line with a group of old trees Go through the gate and left .	
0.1	14.95	Ignore steep track on right and continue ahead as the track starts to get steeper	
0.34	15.29	Left onto wider track - still uphill	
0.18	15.47	Out of woods and left to join another track (Caldron Mill Lane)	
0.17	15.64	Right onto tarmac road (Green Lane)	
0.37	16.01	Turn left signed to Fadmoor	
0.4	16.41	Turn left signed to Fadmoor	
0.06	16.47	Turn right at the Plough public house	
0.53	17	Follow road into Gillamoor passing the Oak Tree public house	
0.27	17.27	Follow the road out of the village passing church on your right	
0.67	17.94	Long fast downhill to meet with a road on your right to Farndale	

| | | LOCATION - BRANSDALE & FARNDALE | DISTANCE |
| 58% OFFROAD | | DIFFICULTY - MEDIUM WITH A FEW LONG CLIMBS | 21.2 MILES |
SPLIT DISTANCE	TOTAL DISTANCE	DESCRIPTION BETWEEN POINTS	DIAGRAM OF LOCATION
0.92	18.86	Turn right onto bridleway	
0.63	19.49	Keep to left of farm	
0.07	19.56	Keep left of open gate and follow track through bracken following a stone wall	
0.3	19.86	Through gate and downhill	
0.13	19.99	Straight ahead at farm on wide stone track going uphill	
0.14	20.13	Turn right onto tarmac road	
1.01	21.14	Ignore road on right	
0.06	21.2	Follow road back to start of route	

Route 4

Kildale, Hob Hole and Baysdale

Total Distance: 17.55 miles   **Offroad:** 67%

Start/Finish: Grid reference 607094 (Kildale)

Start from the tearoom near Kildale railway station. Park in the car park at the Kildale railway station and turn left out of the car park back towards Kildale.

Once you come to the tearoom, reset your trip computer to zero as the mileage readings start here.

Pass the tearoom on your left to join the main road through Kildale village. Turn left at the T-junction and continue along tarmac road. After about 0.33 miles turn right and uphill towards Little Kildale, proceed uphill on this tarmac road (Green Gate Lane) as it passes through Little Kildale Wood. Once out of the wood you come to Warren Farm, just before the farm-house turn right by a line of trees onto a signed bridleway. Pass through a gate then downhill passing an old chimneystack on your left (if you look to the hill ahead of you, you can see the path that you follow as it climbs the hill). Near the bottom of this descent pass a gate on your left and go through gates ahead. As you continue uphill across a field keep to the right following the fence.

Do not go through the gate in the fence but aim for the small gate in the top right-hand corner of the field. Head uphill on a small path and through another gate near the crest of the hill, follow the path over the top and quite steeply downhill to an old ruined barn, go left here and follow a wide track for 1.24 miles until it meets a tarmac road. Turn right onto the road and go steeply downhill to a ford in the bottom of the valley — (Hob Hole, get someone to have a barbecue ready for you). Cross the ford, then continue steeply uphill and take the road off on the right, after 0.3 miles take the bridleway on the right as it climbs uphill, pass a cairn after 0.27 miles then a small steam 0.36 miles later.

Continue along this rocky path (Skinner Howe Cross Road) past another cairn then downhill until you come to a small bridge over Great Hograth Beck. Turn right and follow the beck for a short distance then turn hairpin left and uphill on a wider track, after about 0.4 miles you come to a fork in the track — keep right and slightly uphill. After 0.27 miles pass a large cairn and go downhill to the edge of the wood ahead (Grain Planting East), turn left following the track with the wood on your right for about 200 metres where you come to see a gate on your right that leads into the wood. Turn left here away from the

The ford at Hob Hole can get very deep during long periods
of rain or after snow melts

wood and uphill on a wide track over open moor. Follow this track for about 1 mile where you will see some shooting boxes on your left (U-shaped stone structures about 4 feet high). Stop at the 3rd box (labelled No9) then look across to the right at 90 degrees to the track, you will see a shallow gully in the heather – leave the track and follow this gully across the heather for about 100 metres. Here the track seems to fade, but if you look ahead, you can see the path to join about 250 metres ahead.

When you meet this path, bear right and continue on it for 1.22 miles slightly downhill all the way into the valley bottom (this track can be very wet in winter).

Cross the two small bridges then follow the track uphill again for 0.46 miles until you see a small cairn on your left. Turn left here and follow the track for 0.85 miles over Middle Head Top until you come to a larger cairn at Burton Howe, go ahead to the junction with a wide, stony track and turn right. Follow the wide track downhill for 1.23 miles until you arrive at a Cleveland Way sign, turn right here and downhill again for 0.8 miles until you come to a cross-road with a small cairn on the left. Turn left and take the smaller track as it twists and turns downhill for 0.43 miles. Turn right and join a rough track as it goes downhill on Ingleby Bank or Turkey Nab. Follow the track downhill and though a gate ahead of you and, after 0.41 miles, pass through another gate, pass Bank Foot Farm and cycle onto tarmac.

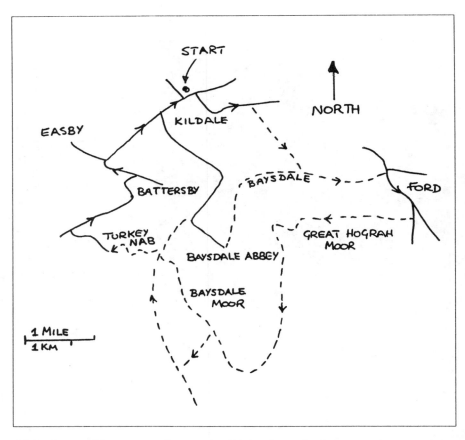

After about 100 metres a "loose road" joins from the left — continue straight ahead for 0.59 miles then turn right towards Kildale, if however you have worked up a thirst turn left and you will see the Dudley Arms on the left-hand side of the road. Follow the Kildale road as it passes though Battersby and crosses a level crossing on the Middlesbrough to Whitby Esk Valley railway line, turn right at the next junction and follow the Kildale road under a railway bridge and into Kildale village. Turn left just after the post-office to return to the start — and a well-deserved pot of tea.

	LOCATION - KILDALE HOB HOLE & BAYSDALE		DISTANCE
67% OFFROAD	DIFFICULTY - MEDIUM, HARD TO FOLLOW IN SNOW		17.55 MILES
SPLIT DISTANCE	TOTAL DISTANCE	DESCRIPTION BETWEEN POINTS	DIAGRAM OF LOCATION
0	0	Start from the tea-room at Kildale Grid Ref. 607094 Car parking at Kildale railway station	
0.33	0.33	Turn right and uphill through trees	
0.87	1.2	Turn right just before Warren Farm onto a bridleway	
0.07	1.27	Through gate and downhill across a field, passing an old chimney stack on your left	
0.24	1.51	Pass gate on your left and then pass through two gates	
0.15	1.66	Continue uphill across field, keep to right and follow the fence . Do not go through the gate into the adjoining field	
0.17	1.83	Through gate in the top corner of the field and then ahead uphill over open moor	
0.22	2.05	Through gate near the top of the hill then continue ahead following the track downhill towards the valley bottom	
0.35	2.4	Turn left at the old ruined barn onto a wider track	
1.24	3.64	Turn right onto tarmac and steeply downhill	
0.27	3.91	Cross the ford at Hob Hole and continue steeply uphill (or take a breather at this popular picnic spot)	
0.32	4.23	Turn right along tarmac road	

SPLIT DISTANCE	TOTAL DISTANCE	LOCATION - KILDALE HOB HOLE & BAYSDALE	DISTANCE
		LOCATION - KILDALE HOB HOLE & BAYSDALE	DISTANCE
67% OFFROAD		DIFFICULTY - MEDIUM, HARD TO FOLLOW IN SNOW	17.55 MILES
SPLIT DISTANCE	TOTAL DISTANCE	DESCRIPTION BETWEEN POINTS	DIAGRAM OF LOCATION
0.3	4.53	Turn right onto bridleway and follow track uphill	
0.27	4.8	Pass a small cairn and continue ahead on small track	
0.32	5.12	Cross small stream	
0.36	5.48	Pass another cairn and continue ahead picking your way around stones,going downhill to a small stream On your right is the path you've just ridden	
0.35	5.83	Cross small bridge over the stream and turn right to meet a well defined track. Turn left and uphill	
0.04	5.87	Continue uphill on a wider track	
0.3	6.17	As moor level out, fork right going slightly uphill	
0.27	6.44	Pass a larger cairn then go downhill through a gap in the dry stone wall and continue to the edge of a wood	
		Continue along the path parrallel with the wood passing a gate on your right	
0.11	6.55	Turn left onto a wide track and uphill over open moor	
1.22	7.77	Follow track until you come to some shooting boxes on your left. Stop at the third box (Labled No9) and you follow a gully in the heather on your right.	
0.2	7.97	Continue across the heather for 100 meters. The path fades to nothing but you can see the path that you join ahead of you	

		LOCATION - KILDALE HOB HOLE & BAYSDALE	DISTANCE
67% OFFROAD		DIFFICULTY - MEDIUM, HARD TO FOLLOW IN SNOW	17.55 MILES
SPLIT DISTANCE	TOTAL DISTANCE	DESCRIPTION BETWEEN POINTS	DIAGRAM OF LOCATION
1.22	9.19	Downhill to the valley bottom, over two stone bridges then uphill again	
0.46	9.65	Turn left near a small cairn	
0.85	10.54	Pass large cairn and continue ahead to a junction. Turn right onto a wide stony track	
1.23	11.86	Going mostly downhill, turn right at the Cleveland Way sign	
0.8	12.66	Left onto a small track	
0.43	13.09	Join rough track and go right downhill from Turkey Nab	
0.24	13.33	Through gate	
0.41	13.74	Through gate and pass Bank Foot Farm onto tarmac	
0.1	13.84	Left at junction	
0.59	14.43	Turn right towards Kildale with the Dudley Arms public house on your left and follow the road through Battersby village 0.9 miles further on	
1.81	16.24	Turn right towards Kildale	
1.31	17.55	Turn left back to the tea-room	

Route 5

Glaisdale

Total Distance: 10.78 miles   **Offroad:** 66%

Start/Finish: Grid reference 779036 (Glaisdale Rigg)

Start from the gravel car park on Glaisdale Rigg. This is the road that runs between Egton Bridge and Rosedale. The car park is located about 2 miles from Egton Bridge just after a cattle grid.

Turn right out of the car park and continue uphill on tarmac. After 0.78 miles pass a footpath on the right, then a bridleway on the right 0.59 miles further on. Continue on tarmac with Wintergill Plantation on your right. About 300 metres after the plantation ends turn right onto a bridleway. The track follows a gully in the moor. Follow the gully for 0.65 miles. Go through a gate and follow the path as the gully starts to level out and sweep round to the right. Follow the path downhill towards a dry stone wall next to a wood. Go to an iron gate in the wall where you should see the track bend to the left, following another gully downhill. The track doubles back on itself and continues downhill where it comes to a wooden gate in a wall. Go through this gate and across a field to a gate in the bottom. Turn left at Mountain Ash Farm onto tarmac and follow the road downhill to the bottom of the valley, then uphill passing a house with well kept garden, and past Yew Grange Farm. After passing the farm cross a bridge and turn left on a single track road signposted to Rosedale. Follow the tarmac track uphill for 0.23 miles then turn right through a gate at a bridleway sign.

Continue through another gate then over a river. Follow the wall on your left past a ruined building. Pass a gate on your right, then go through the gate ahead of you. Turn right before the next gate and follow the dry stone wall on your right-hand side. (There should be a row of trees on the left-hand side of the field that you are in). Continue up the field until you come to a gate in the wall. Carry on past this gate until you come to a second. Go through this gate and follow the track as it first goes straight ahead then curves round to the left, crosses the field. Continue to a gate in the top left corner of the field. Do not go through this gate, but go up the steps in the wall at the head of the field. Follow the path ahead with Highdale Farm being on your left on the other side of the wall. After about 50 metres turn left through a gate in the wall then turn immediately right. Go through the gate ahead of you and then continue on this track for about 300 metres until you come to a junction with a tarmac road.

Turn right along tarmac for a short distance and take the wide grassy track on your left. Follow this until it meets another tarmac road near a cattle grid. Turn right here onto the road and uphill to some crossroads on top of the ridge. Go straight ahead here on a wide stony track as it goes downhill along Glaisdale side for about 0.5 miles where you come to another crossroads. Bear left here for 300 metres then take a right turn onto another wide track. After 250

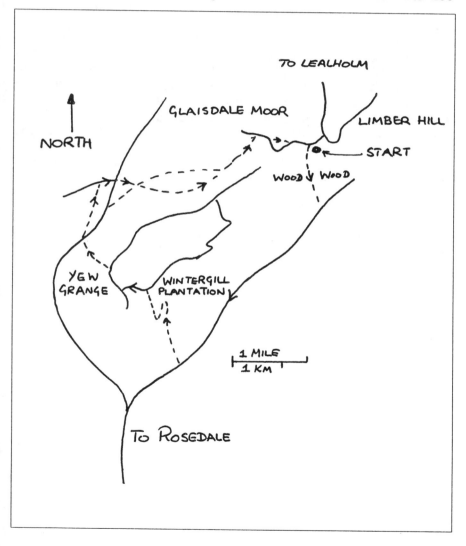

metres a track joins from the right. Continue straight ahead downhill here for a quarter of a mile to a small stone bridge that can be easily missed. Once you've found the bridge (overlooking Postgate Farm) cross it and turn left on a small track that goes steeply uphill. Follow this track around to the left of the mound ahead of you, then continue uphill keeping to the track right around the top of an old quarry.

Continue on this track as it goes left keeping to the right of the stone wall. Proceed along this track across the moor, where after 0.45 miles you come to a bridleway sign on your left. Bear left by this sign for about 200 metres where you come to a second bridleway sign. Go straight ahead at this sign for 0.26 miles, through a gate and onto tarmac. Follow this road for a further 0.46 miles to a T-junction by a small green. Take a right turn here and continue downhill into Glaisdale. (Refreshments in the Mytre Tavern perhaps?)

Take the road that is opposite the pub and is signed "Local Traffic"; there is a telephone box on the corner. Follow this road downhill for 0.53 miles until you come to a T-junction near the Arncliffe Arms. Go left and downhill at this junction towards Glaisdale station and the Station tearooms. Just before the railway bridge turn right over a ford along a track signed "Unsuitable for motors". After about 200 metres there is a gated track on your right — keep *left* here and ride uphill along the edge of Arncliff Woods. After 0.57 miles you come back onto tarmac and pass Snowdon Nab Farm. Continue ahead for 0.23 miles to a T-junction on the Egton to Rosedale road, turn right here and gently uphill for 0.48 miles back to the start.

	LOCATION - GLAISDALE		DISTANCE
66% OFFROAD	DIFFICULTY - MEDIUM		10.78 MILES

SPLIT DISTANCE	TOTAL DISTANCE	DESCRIPTION BETWEEN POINTS	DIAGRAM OF LOCATION
0	0	Start from car park on the Glaisdale to Rosedale road at Grid Ref. 779036 Turn right out of car park and uphill	
0.78	0.78	Stay on tarmac passing a signed footpath on your right	
0.59	1.37	Pass bridleway on your right just before you come to the woods	
0.36	1.73	Pass a footpath on your left keeping the wood on your right	
0.37	2.1	Pass footpath on your right	
0.11	2.21	Turn right onto a bridleway as it follows a gully across the moor	
0.65	2.86	Go through a gate and follow the path as the gully starts to level out and sweep round to the right. Go downhill to the stone wall next to the wood	
0.23	3.09	Go to the iron gate in the wall, do not go through the gate but follow the track to the left and downhill following another gully	
0.19	3.28	Continue downhill to a wooden gate and go through it	
0.11	3.39	Cross a field then through a gate at the bottom. Turn left at Mountain Ash Farm following tarmac downhill then uphill passing Yew Grange Farm	
0.77	4.16	Pass farm then over a bridge, turn left onto the single track road signed to Rosedale	
0.23	4.39	Uphill to bridleway sign. Turn right through a gate then across a field	

SPLIT DISTANCE	TOTAL DISTANCE	DESCRIPTION BETWEEN POINTS	DIAGRAM OF LOCATION
LOCATION - GLAISDALE			DISTANCE
66% OFFROAD		DIFFICULTY - MEDIUM	10.78 MILES
0.08	4.47	Through gate and over a river	
0.1	4.57	Follow wall on left passing a ruined building. Pass a gate on your right then go through the gate ahead. Turn right before the next gate following wall on your right	
0.15	4.72	Go through the second gate in the wall and follow the track ahead as it curves to the left	
0.13	4.85	Continue on path as it around to the left and across the field to the top left corner next to a blue wooden pole Go up steps in the wall and uphill with house on your left	
0.08	4.93	Continue alongside the wall for 50 metres then through a gate on your left, turn right and through another gate. Follow tarmac track across the moor	
0.21	5.14	Turn right on tarmac road	
0.04	5.18	Take the track on your left	
0.68	5.86	Right onto tarmac and uphill with cattle grid on your left	
0.11	5.97	Follow road uphill ignoring the track ahead	
0.18	6.15	Cross road and onto a wide track	
0.49	6.64	Bear left at crossroads	
0.15	6.79	Keep right at junction	

		LOCATION - GLAISDALE	DISTANCE
66% OFFROAD		DIFFICULTY - MEDIUM	10.78 MILES

SPLIT DISTANCE	TOTAL DISTANCE	DESCRIPTION BETWEEN POINTS	DIAGRAM OF LOCATION
0.13	6.92	Ignore track joining from right	
0.25	7.17	Downhill and over stone bridge then steeply uphill Note It is quite easy to miss this junction if you are not looking out for it	
0.04	7.21	Keep left at junction, keeping left of the mound ahead of you	
0.05	7.26	Continue on track as it follows the top edge of an small quarry. The track then goes left following a dry stone wall across the moor	
0.45	7.71	At bridleway sign take the track that bears left at a lower level and not the track that goes straight ahead	
0.07	7.78	Go straight ahead at this second bridleway sign and ignore the track on your left	
0.26	8.04	Through gate and onto tarmac	
0.46	8.5	Turn right onto tarmac and downhill towards Glaisdale	
0.15	8.65	Turn left opposite the Mytre Tavern between a phone box and a local traffic sign and go downhill	
0.53	9.18	Turn left at the junction near to the Arncliffe Arms public house	
0.11	9.29	Continue downhill to Glaisdale station passing the Beggars Bridge tea-room (or going in) and public toilets	
0.06	9.35	Just before the railway bridge turn right and cross the river ford. Note If you want to extend the ride you can detour on routes 10 & 11 which will return you here	

		LOCATION - GLAISDALE	DISTANCE
66% OFFROAD		DIFFICULTY - MEDIUM	10.78 MILES

SPLIT DISTANCE	TOTAL DISTANCE	DESCRIPTION BETWEEN POINTS	DIAGRAM OF LOCATION
0.07	9.42	Follow track marked "unsuitable for motors" then keep left uphill	
0.08	9.5	Keep left and uphill	
0.57	10.07	Pass farmhouse and onto tarmac	
0.23	10.3	Right at junction	
0.48	10.78	Uphill and over cattle grid and back to the start	CAR PARK

Route 6

Aislby, Grosmont and Egton

Total Distance: 16.62 miles   **Offroad:** 60%

Start/Finish: Grid reference 857086 (Aislby)

Start is at Aislby, from the bus stop close to the war memorial. Take the signed bridleway opposite the bus stop and after about 0.25 miles turn right onto a track towards Home Farm. After another 0.3 miles ignore a track on your right but continue around to your left. About 60 metres further on ignore the track on your right. Now go downhill for 0.33 miles passing Lodge Farm on your left. Just after the farmhouse turn right through a gate and across fields. Go through two more gates and towards a small wood (Back Wood), cross a footbridge and turn right.

You soon come to a tarmac road. Cross this road, a sign to Grosmont and follow the stone path through four gates for about 0.4 miles and into Hecks Wood. Continue on this path as it goes right and slightly uphill for about 0.25 miles, then through a gate and out of the wood. Go though two more gates and pass Newbiggin Hall Farm on your left. A quarter of a mile after the farm, bear left through a gate onto a stone path signed to Grosmont. After about 250 metres you come to a gate, pass through and continue left around the outside of a field with Cote Bank Wood on your left. Go through another gate then downhill into the wood. About 400 metres further on though another gate, turn right over a ford and then along a wide track past Grosmont farm to a junction with a tarmac road. Go left, and after passing some houses on your right, come to a junction with the Egton to Grosmont road. Turn left towards Grosmont – about 30 metres further on there is a track on the right, signed 'Egton 1 mile'.

The route continues along this track, however if you are in need of refreshment, miss this track on your right and instead continue along the tarmac road towards Grosmont. Pass the cricket field and head towards the village. There is a tearoom on your right, or continue over the level crossing to the Station Hotel – I've also heard that the tea in the North York Moors Railway station cafe is quite good!

If you have been into Grosmont retrace your steps (or tracks) back to the wide track signed to Egton. Follow this track for about 1 mile as it goes under a bridge and passes Egton Manor. When you come to a junction with a tarmac road you come to the start of a long stretch of road work, with the next mile being uphill. Turn right uphill passing the Church, continue past a road on the right to Grosmont, and about 250 metres further on pass a road on the left to Glaisdale. Just opposite the second pub on your right (Horseshoe), take the road that forks left signed to Guisborough and follow this for 1.25 miles to a cross-roads. Turn right and continue to a T-junction, this time with the main Guisborough to Whitby road. Take care on this busy road as you turn right towards Whitby for about 500 metres until you reach a track on the left with a bridleway sign.

Cross open fields for about 600 metres then go through a gate and ahead again. After a further 500 metres go through another gate then turn right following the edge of a field near to a bridleway sign. Go through the gate into Folly Wood, and follow the path downhill over a small bridge and through another gate. Now turn left through a second gate and follow the waymarker uphill. At the top of the rise cross the style on your left into the adjacent field and turn right, you should now have the fence on your right. After 200 metres go though a gate on your right and back into the original field. Turn left and

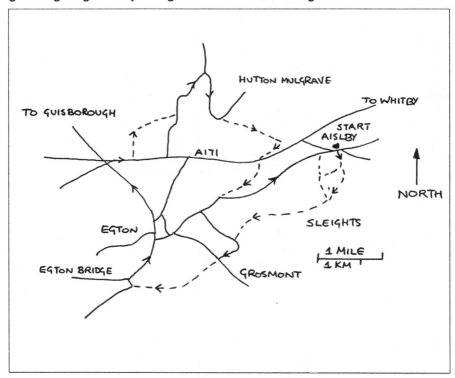

continue ahead towards Brisco Farm. After about 400 metres pass through a gate, 200 metres further on go through two more gates keeping to the right of Brisco Farm.

Turn left onto the tarmac road and ride for about 1 mile to a T-junction. Go right here along a straight road, passing Moorgate Farm and sweeping left after about 0.7 miles. About 500 metres after the farm the road turns sharp left. Take the signed bridleway that goes straight ahead towards Hutton Mulgrave Woods.

Follow the track into the woods and stay on the main track for about 0.75 miles where you come to a wireless station on your right, turning right here passing the wireless station building. Stay on this track for about 200 metres to a fire break. Cross the break by going left then immediately right and back into the wood. Follow the track until it emerges from the wood. If you look across to your right, you should be able to see a gate on the far side of the field. After passing through the gate turn right taking care on the main Guisborough to Whitby road, and after 250 metres follow the signed bridleway down a wide track towards Moorcock Farm.

Just in front of the farmhouse go through a small gate on your left, then turn right and around the back of the house to another gate. As you pass through the gate look ahead towards the wood ahead of you and make for the top right-hand edge of it keeping towards the top of the field. Close to the top of the wood is a gate in the dry stone wall. Go through the gate going slightly left and downhill on a grassy track through the wood. Stay on the track as you emerge from the wood passing Top Stone Farm on your right.

Continue on this track for another 0.5 miles to a junction with a tarmac road at Coopers Farm. Turn left here and follow the road for 2.2 miles back to the start.

	LOCATION - AISLBY, GROSMONT AND EGTON		DISTANCE
60% OFFROAD	DIFFICULTY - MEDIUM		16.648 MILES

SPLIT DISTANCE	TOTAL DISTANCE	DESCRIPTION BETWEEN POINTS	DIAGRAM OF LOCATION
0	0	Start at Aislby at Grid Ref.857086 - Park in village close to the War Memorial. Take the bridleway opposite the bus shelter (near the War Memorial)	
0.27	0.27	Turn right	
0.3	0.57	Turn left then ignore track on your right	
0.36	0.93	Pass house on hill and turn right through a gate going across fields through two more gates	
0.22	1.15	Over small bridge and into wood	
0.12	1.27	Turn right while in the wood	
0.03	1.3	Cross tarmac road following a sign to Grosmont	
0.19	1.49	Through three gates within a few hundred metres of each other	
0.34	1.83	Through gate and into Hecks Wood	
0.24	2.07	Through three more gates then pass Newbiggin Hall Farm on your left	
0.3	2.47	Turn left through a gate onto a path signed to Grosmont	
0.13	2.6	Through gate and follow path around left hand side of field with woods on your left	

		LOCATION - AISLBY, GROSMONT AND EGTON	DISTANCE
60% OFFROAD		DIFFICULTY - MEDIUM	16.648 MILES
SPLIT DISTANCE	TOTAL DISTANCE	DESCRIPTION BETWEEN POINTS	DIAGRAM OF LOCATION
0.14	2.74	Through gate and downhill through woods	
0.21	2.95	Through gate then keep right and over a ford	
0.71	3.66	Pass Grosmont Farm and follow wide track to a junction with tarmac and continue ahead.	
0.31	3.97	Meet the Egton to Grosmont road. Turn left then right on a track signed to Egton Bridge	
**	**	You could continue ahead into Grosmont here if required for a pot of tea in Grosmont village	
0.53	4.5	Under railway bridge	
0.94	5.44	Pass Egton Manor then turn right and steeply uphill on tarmac towards Egton village passing the church halfway up the bank	
0.98	6.42	Pass road on your right to Grosmont	
0.13	6.55	Pass two pubs and turn left opposite the garage	
1.31	7.86	Turn right at the crossroads	
0.18	8.04	Take care as you briefly join the Whitby Guisborough road.	
0.39	8.43	Take signed bridleway on left over open field	

		LOCATION - AISLBY, GROSMONT AND EGTON	DISTANCE
60% OFFROAD		DIFFICULTY - MEDIUM	16.648 MILES
SPLIT DISTANCE	TOTAL DISTANCE	DESCRIPTION BETWEEN POINTS	DIAGRAM OF LOCATION
0.39	8.82	Through gate	
0.31	9.13	Through gate and turn right following the edge of the field then through a second gate and into the wood	
0.13	9.26	Over bridge and follow signs, through two gates and uphill. At top of hill cross a stile on your left following the fence that is now on your right	
0.15	9.41	Through gate and back into the first field !!	
0.29	9.7	Pass through three gates keeping to the right of the farm and onto tarmac road	
1.07	10.77	Right at T junction	
1.05	11.82	Straight ahead on signed bridleway	
0.22	12.04	Straight ahead into wood	
0.1	12.14	Ignore track on right	
0.21	12.35	Ahead at crossroads	
0.3	12.65	Cross fire break	
0.12	12.77	Turn right after radio transmitter	

		LOCATION - AISLBY, GROSMONT AND EGTON	DISTANCE
60% OFFROAD		DIFFICULTY - MEDIUM	16.648 MILES
SPLIT DISTANCE	TOTAL DISTANCE	DESCRIPTION BETWEEN POINTS	DIAGRAM OF LOCATION
0.13	12.9	Cross fire break	
0.1	13	Out of wood and bear right over the field towards a gate on the far side	
0.09	13.09	Through gate onto the main Guisborough to Whitby road	
0.11	13.2	Turn left onto track down to Moorcock Farm	
0.12	13.32	Turn left through gate just before the farmhouse and around the back of the house to another gate	
0.06	13.38	Through gate then across field towards the top right hand corner (Top of the wood) to a gate in the dry stone wall	
0.27	13.65	Through gate and into the wood, continue downhill through wood on grassy track. Pass out of the wood and then towards the farm	
0.32	13.97	Pass farm on your right hand side	
0.46	14.43	Turn left onto tarmac and follow the road back to start	
2.21	16.64	End	

Route 7

Kilburn and Boltby

Total Distance: 13.24 miles   **Offroad:** 65%

Start/Finish: Grid reference 515831 (Sutton Bank Visitor Centre)

Start from the visitor centre at the top of Sutton Bank where there is ample car parking together with public conveniences and tearoom.

Leave the car park by turning left onto the main Thirsk to Scarborough road – taking care on this often very busy main road. After 0.25 miles turn right onto a tarmac road until you come to an "unsuitable for motors" sign. Continue ahead on this wide track (Hightown Bank Road) with woods on your right. Continue on this track for 1.27 miles as it sweeps downhill through woods until it meets a tarmac road. Turn right onto the tarmac and ignoring the junction on your left, continue downhill for 0.5 miles to another road junction. Turn right here for about 200 metres, then turn left onto a bridleway. Follow this bridleway next to fields then uphill through Hoodhill Plantation. When you arrive at a junction with a wide forest track go left onto a good downhill stretch for 0.27 miles. You should see a junction with a similar wide track on your right (if you look to your right you will be able to see the crags of Ivy Scar). Do not go right here but continue ahead and slightly uphill. After 0.24 miles look for a bridleway sign on the right and follow this signed track along the side of the wood then over fields towards Hood Grange Farm.

Just before the farm buildings turn left to a small footbridge at the end of the field, cross the bridge and continue ahead until you meet the main farm track. Go left here and follow this track to the Thirsk-Scarbrough road. Go left here onto the main road, taking care as this can be very busy – particularly in summer.

After about 25 metres turn right onto a wide bridleway. Follow the track for 250 metres where another bridleway sign leads you right then left between two wire fences. Continue along here as it turns to the left through a gate and to the left of a small lake – Cleaves Wood Farm is on your left. Next follow the waymarked track on the right and through another gate, coming to two footpath signs on the left and right – ignore these and continue ahead passing a small wooden barn on your right. Go across fields and through two more gates to Cleaves House. Keep right of the house and you come to a tarmac road.

Turn right onto tarmac for 0.25 miles to Southlands Lodge. Turn left just after the house through a gate and onto a good wide track—you have now covered 5.87 miles. Follow the track for 0.38 miles through a gate to crossroads. Go straight on at this junction for about 200 metres then follow a grassy track on the left that is signposted to Tang Hall. Follow the path through two gates across fields for about 0.5 miles until you see a line of poles across a field. Follow this line then pick up the track that bears left to Tang Hall Farm 0.25 miles away. From Tang Hall turn right over a cattle grid for 0.4 miles to Green-

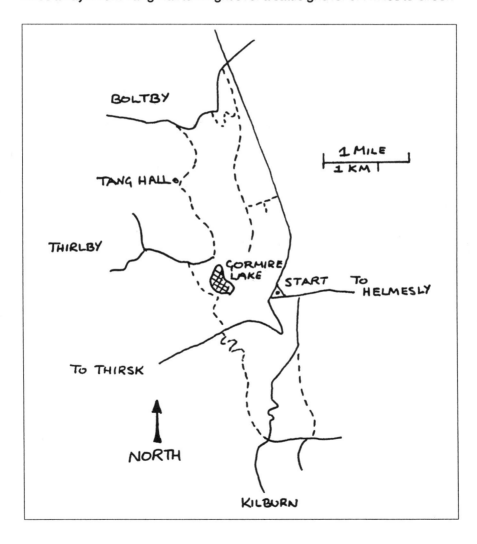

dale Farm. Pass to the left of the farm through a gate and across a small field to a small gate at the far side. Go through this gate, turn left and head uphill through trees for about 0.2 miles.

After going through a gate follow the track left signposted to Boltby. Go through another gate then downhill across a field for 0.2 miles though another gate and onto a wider track. Follow this over a footbridge and onto tarmac to a junction with another road – Boltby church should be on your right. Go right here following the road for 0.6 miles as it passes a water treatment works. After the works the road turns sharp left – go straight ahead here though a gate following the bridleway sign as the path zigzags uphill (do not go into the wood) to the top of the ridge ahead. Once you get to the top you come to a building (High Barn). Turn right here and follow the path along the top edge of the cliff.

After about 200 metres go through a small gate keeping left of the stone wall, after 0.26 miles go through another small gate and continue on the track ahead. After 0.44 miles you come to a bridleway sign on the left. Ignore this and continue ahead for a further 0.38 miles to another bridleway sign, this sign being next to a gate stood alone with no fence or wall near it. Go left here across fields for about 0.5 miles until you meet a tarmac road (ignore the bridleway sign pointing right halfway to the road) Turn right onto tarmac road and follow it past a radio mast until you come to a T-junction. Turn right here and follow the road for a further 0.8 miles back to the car park.

		LOCATION - KILBURN AND BOLTBY	DISTANCE
		DIFFICULTY - FAIRLY EASY	
65% OFFROAD			13.24 MILES

SPLIT DISTANCE	TOTAL DISTANCE	DESCRIPTION BETWEEN POINTS	DIAGRAM OF LOCATION
0	0	Start from the café at the top of Sutton Bank Grid Ref. 515831 Turn left onto the Scarborough road	
0.25	0.25	Turn right staying on tarmac	
0.48	0.73	Bear left at "unsuitable for motors sign and follow a good track through woods	
1.27	2	Turn right onto tarmac after the good downhill and ignore the road on your left	
0.53	2.53	Turn sharp right	
0.1	2.63	Left onto bridleway and uphill through woods	
0.64	3.27	Bear left in woods onto a wide forest track downhill	
0.27	3.54	Continue ahead with crags high on your right	
0.24	3.78	Take signed bridleway on your right through wood then across fields towards the farm	
0.22	4	Turn left in front of farm before the fence	
0.11	4.11	Turn right through gate and then cross over a bridge, continue straight ahead.	
0.05	4.16	Through gate then left on wide farm track	

LOCATION - KILBURN AND BOLTBY			DISTANCE	
65% OFFROAD		DIFFICULTY - FAIRLY EASY	13.24 MILES	
SPLIT DISTANCE	TOTAL DISTANCE	DESCRIPTION BETWEEN POINTS	DIAGRAM OF LOCATION	
0.37	4.53	**Left onto main road with caution**	
0.1	4.63	Turn right onto a bridleway	
0.16	4.79	Follow bridleway between two fences and through a gate	
0.17	4.96	Through gate	
0.16	5.12	Pass between farm and small lake	
0.17	5.29	Follow waymark sign through gate then ignore footpath signs on right and left. Continue ahead with small wooden building on your right	
0.12	5.41	Through gate and across field	
0.1	5.51	Through gate and pass farm on your left	
0.11	5.62	Pass house on left then turn right through gate	
0.25	5.87	Left after house and through gate along a good track	
0.38	6.25	Through gate and continue straight ahead	
0.09	6.34	Ahead following the sign for Tang Hall on a grass track	

	LOCATION - KILBURN AND BOLTBY		DISTANCE
65% OFFROAD	DIFFICULTY - FAIRLY EASY		13.24 MILES

SPLIT DISTANCE	TOTAL DISTANCE	DESCRIPTION BETWEEN POINTS	DIAGRAM OF LOCATION
0.08	6.42	Through gate and across field	
0.15	6.57	Through gate and across field	
0.13	6.7	Turn right and follow line of poles across field	
0.28	6.98	Through gate and pass Tang Hall farm then right over a cattle grid towards Greendale	
0.42	7.4	Pass Greendale farm then through gate over a field	
0.05	7.45	Through gate then uphill through trees	
0.31	7.76	Through gate and left towards Boltby and then through gate and downhill across field	
0.2	7.96	Through gate and along a wide track towards a footbridge	
0.27	8.23	Cross footbridge	
0.31	8.54	Turn right with church on your right	
0.6	9.14	Through gate and onto bridleway	
0.09	9.23	Through gate	

		LOCATION - KILBURN AND BOLTBY	DISTANCE
65% OFFROAD		DIFFICULTY - FAIRLY EASY	13.24 MILES

SPLIT DISTANCE	TOTAL DISTANCE	DESCRIPTION BETWEEN POINTS	DIAGRAM OF LOCATION
0.11	9.34	Take left hairpin before gate	
0.13	9.47	Turn right and uphill before the farm	
0.08	9.55	Track turns left and follows a row of trees	
0.1	9.65	Turn right just before the wall near and old tree trunk	
0.08	9.73	Through gate and turn right	
0.04	9.77	Follow zigzag track uphill towards trees on the brow	
0.15	9.92	Right at High Barn and follow the track along the cliff edge	
0.18	10.1	Keep to left of wall and through gate	
0.26	10.36	Gate	
0.54	10.9	Ahead at bridleway sign - do not turn left here	
0.38	11.28	Follow bridleway across field next to a gate on it's own with no fences near it	
0.25	11.32	Ignore signed track on your right	

		LOCATION - KILBURN AND BOLTBY	DISTANCE
65% OFFROAD		DIFFICULTY - FAIRLY EASY	13.24 MILES
SPLIT DISTANCE	TOTAL DISTANCE	DESCRIPTION BETWEEN POINTS	DIAGRAM OF LOCATION
0.25	11.78	Turn right onto tarmac	
		Pass radio mast on your left	
0.6	12.38	Turn right at T junction	
0.86	13.24	Finish at car park and tea-room	CAR PARK

Route 8

Robin Hood's Bay and Sneaton

Total Distance: 15.24 miles   **Offroad:** 73%

Start/Finish: Grid reference 905055 (Robin Hood's Bay — Coach and Car Park)

Start from the coach and car park at Robin Hood's Bay leaving on a road directly opposite the entrance to the car park and following a sign pointing out the Cleveland Way. Follow this road to the end turning sharp left. Pass a house on your right and ignoring the first track on your right follow the track signed "Railway Path". Do not follow the "Cleveland Way" sign.

Stay on this track as it goes slightly uphill for about 2.5 miles. It's worth mentioning the spectacular views out to sea and along the coast towards Whitby. When you come to a tarmac road cross it and continue on the railway track. Just after passing under a bridge, you come to the main Whitby to Scarborough road. Take care as you cross this busy road and continue along the old railway track on the other side. After about 0.7 miles you pass under a bridge. Cross over an unusual bridge with wooden support beams and buckled steel plates 0.22 miles further on. Go downhill through woods for 1.34 miles until you cross another bridge over a tarmac road (ahead of you the track is fenced off with steel railings). Immediately after crossing this bridge take the small track on your left down to the road.

Do not go back under the bridge, but coast downhill on tarmac road taking care on the tight corners as they are blind for cars coming towards you. After you have crossed the small river in the bottom of the dip, go uphill until you come to a road off on your left (with a "dead end" sign). Go left here on a road that takes you uphill towards Golden Grove. After passing Shawn Riggs Farm on the right, continue ahead for about 300 metres where, just before the road sweeps to the right you will see a wide track on your right between two hedges. Take this track (with flagstones on the right-hand side) as it goes down into Toppings Wood. Cross two footbridges then uphill on Monks Walk where you pass through a gate and onto a tarmac road. You have now ridden 6.96 miles.

Turn left and continue along the road, on your left is Beacon Farm tearoom. Here you can get not only the usual liquid refreshments but also wonderful home-made ice cream. The Wilson Arms is also handy for anyone who fancies a quick pint.

After your refreshment stop continue on the road with the Wilson arms on your left. After about 0.46 miles you pass two footpath signs and Bennison View on your left. Continue downhill for about 250 metres where you come to some white road-posts on your left. Take the unsigned path off on your right. After about 100 metres ignore a bridleway sign that points to the right.

Continue on the main path as it gets quite rough going downhill into Ford Rigg Mill Wood. At the bottom of the hill, follow the path as it turns right and follows the path of the stream. Continue over a footbridge and uphill to a junction with a wider track. Turn **right** here as the track to the left is not public right of way. This track now continues slightly uphill for 0.47 miles and exits the wood with fields on your left. Stay on the main track ahead through three gates to a junction with tarmac road.

Turn left onto the road and 0.2 miles further on bear left on the road signed to Hawsker. Ignoring the bridleway sign on your right, continue ahead for 0.59

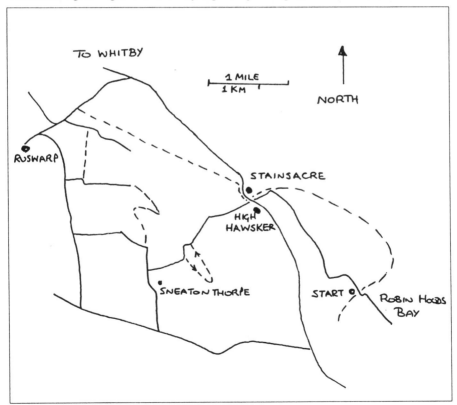

miles until the road turns sharp left. At this turning take the track on your left and follow it for 0.34 miles to a gate. Go through the gate and keep left, pass by a gate on your left and go through the one ahead of you into a field. Follow the field perimeter with a wire fence on your left for about 250 metres. You will now see a gate in the fence on your left, go through the gate and downhill on a wide track for over half a mile.

When the track meets the tarmac road, turn right. After 0.32 miles, you come to a road on your left, ignore this road and continue ahead here for another half mile where you meet the Whitby — Scarborough road again. Go straight across the main road and ahead into the village of Hawsker. Take two left turns straight after each other so you are on the road sign posted to Whitby. Follow this road past the Hare and Hounds pub and take the signed bridleway on the right. Follow the bridleway for about 200 metres and as it crosses the old railway line go over the stile on the right and onto the old line. Do not go under the bridge but turn left and follow the old track on a good downhill back to the car park.

SPLIT DISTANCE	TOTAL DISTANCE	DESCRIPTION BETWEEN POINTS	DIAGRAM OF LOCATION
		LOCATION - ROBIN HOODS BAY AND SNEATON DISTANCE	
		73% OFFROAD DIFFICULTY - EASY 15.24 MILES	
0	0	Start from the coach and car park in Robin Hoods bay. Grid Ref. 950055 and leave on the road opposite the entrance on a road signed "Cleveland Way"	
0.15	0.15	Follow the "Railway Path" and not the Cleveland Way and along the old railway line (the Cleveland Way follows the cliff path)	
2.39	2.54	Stay on the old railway line as it goes gently uphill Cross tarmac road	
0.46	3	Ride under bridge	
0.17	3.17	Take care crossing the Whitby to Scarborough road	
0.69	3.86	Ride under bridge	
0.22	4.08	Over bridge with wooden beams and steel plates	
1.34	5.42	downhill through woods then cross bridge. Just over the bridge turn left down some steps and onto the road Turn right and downhill on tarmac	
0.4	5.82	Take care on this road as it continues downhill and over river. Turn left on road with a dead end sign.	
0.24	6.06	Pass Shaw Riggs farm on your right	
0.12	6.18	Turn right 300 meters after the farm onto a wide track between hedges	
0.27	6.45	Follow track down into Topping Riggs wood over a footbridge then uphill on "Monks Walk"	

SPLIT DISTANCE	TOTAL DISTANCE	DESCRIPTION BETWEEN POINTS	DIAGRAM OF LOCATION
	LOCATION - ROBIN HOODS BAY AND SNEATON	DISTANCE
73% OFFROAD		DIFFICULTY - EASY	15.24 MILES
0.51	6.96	Through gate and left onto tarmac	
0.11	7.07	Beacon Farm tea-room and ice-cream parlor on your left is worth a stop Wilson Arms on your left	
0.46	7.53	Pass two footpath signs and then Bennison View House	
0.12	7.65	Turn right 250 meters after house opposite some white reflective road posts on an unsigned bridleway	
0.06	7.71	After 100 metres ignore track on right	
0.47	8.18	Downhill on rough track into Ford Rigg Mill wood. Near valley bottom follow track going right and follows the river. Over bridge and uphill, turn right at junction	
0.47	8.65	Out of wood with fields on left	
0.28	8.93	Through gate	
'0.18	9.11	Through two gates and left onto tarmac	
0.2	9.31	Follow road signed to Hawsker	
0:13	9.43	Ignore bridleway sign and contine ahead	
0.59	10.02	Turn right onto wide track	

	LOCATION - ROBIN HOODS BAY AND SNEATON		DISTANCE
73% OFFROAD	DIFFICULTY - EASY		15.24 MILES
SPLIT DISTANCE	TOTAL DISTANCE	DESCRIPTION BETWEEN POINTS	DIAGRAM OF LOCATION
0.34	10.36	Through gate and turn left through gorse bushes	
0.04	10.4	Pass gate on left then through gate ahead. Follow wire fence along the left of field	
0.12	10.52	Left onto wide track downhill to tarmac road	
0.61	11.13	Turn right onto tarmac	
0.32	11.45	Ignore track on left	
0.49	11.94	Cross main road	
0.06	12	Left then left again on road signed to Whitby	
0.12	12.12	Turn right on bridleway after the Hare and Hounds pub	
0.12	12.24	Over bridge and stile then right onto the railway line. Turn left towards Robin Hoods Bay Do not go right under the bridge	
3	15.24	Follow track back to the car and coach park	

Route 9

Robin Hood's Bay and Ravenscar

Total Distance: 11.54 miles　　　　　　　　　　　　　**Offroad:** 73%

Start/Finish: Grid reference 950050 (Robin Hood's Bay — Coach and Car Park)

Start from the coach and car park at Robin Hood's Bay, grid reference 950055. Leave towards the village hall with the toilet block on your right. Follow tarmac road downhill, passing the hall to a junction with the Robin Hood's Bay to Fylingthorpe road. Turn right for about 0.5 miles to a cross-roads with a church on the far-left corner. Go straight ahead here, through Fylingthorpe village, then uphill for about 0.5 miles. As the road starts to wind more steeply uphill, look for a road on your left sign posted unsuitable for long vehicles. Soon afterwards, bear left following a YHA sign, towards Fylinghall School. As you see the school building on your left, look right and you should see a signed bridleway track uphill through some Woods (High Park Wood). Take this easy to follow track as it opens out to fields on the right. Continue on the track going back into a wood (Oakwood) and head downhill into Ramsdale passing two houses. Go uphill through a gate into Carr Wood and follow a stony track with a wire fence on your right. After about 400 metres, go through another gate. This track can get very muddy in winter.

After 600 metres you exit the wood at the junction with a path going left, sign-posted to Fylingthorpe Hall. Go left and through a gate following the side of a field with a wall on your right. At the end of the field go right and through another gate signposted to Fylingthorpe Old Hall. Follow the track for 400 metres to another gate. Go through the gate and down hill for 400 metres and passing through another gate by Swallow Head Farm. Pass the farm on your right, and go downhill through a gate onto a tarmac road.

Continued downhill to a T-junction at Fyling Old Hall Farm. Turn right and follow the road round a sharp left-hand bend. Go downhill passing an old Railway track, first on your left, and then your right. (You will return along this Railway track and cross the road later in this route). Continue uphill, ignoring the tarmac road joining from the right.

About 100 metres after this junction look for a bridleway on the right, just opposite a house (painted white when I last passed it). Take the bridleway through trees and downhill over a ford (or over the bridge if you are a wimp).

Turn left and through a gate and follow the track uphill to another gate. Go through this one and again uphill towards the buildings ahead.

When you come to the old Railway line, cross it by going through a gate to Brownside farm. Turn left immediately after this gate. Follow the track for a few metres as it turns to the right. Turn left and go through another gate and follow this track in front of the house then around to the right as it passes a stable or barn on the left.

Continue up the hill, through a gate, then left onto a white loose gravel track. After about 0.4 miles, the track joins with a tarmac road. Continue straight ahead following the tarmac road up Stoupe Brow for about half a mile. Turn left at a bridleway sign and follow a small track downhill. As the track widens,

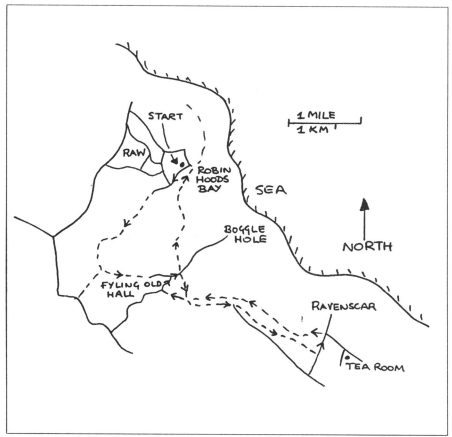

continue straight ahead where the loose surface turns to tarmac. After about 500 metres you come to a T-junction.

If you want to take a break for a cup of tea and a piece of cake, turn right and uphill for 400 metres to the Smugglers Rock Tearoom. If not go left here and go downhill into Ravenscar and the National Trust coastal station.

Turn left downhill, passing the coastal station. After 150 metres, turn left to join the old railway track and pass under two bridges. Continue on the railway path for about another 2 miles until you come to a tarmac road (the one you came down earlier). To cross it, first go left up the road for a few metres, then back onto the track. Stay on this track for about 1 mile and cross the tarmac road near the cricket field. Stay on the track for 0.75 miles to a junction with a tarmac road, turn right for about 50 metres, and then left. Go back to the car park on the road signposted to the village Hall.

SPLIT DISTANCE	TOTAL DISTANCE	DESCRIPTION BETWEEN POINTS	DIAGRAM OF LOCATION
		LOCATION - ROBIN HOODS BAY AND RAVENSCAR DISTANCE	
73% OFFROAD		DIFFICULTY - EASY 11.54 MILES	
0	0	Start from the coach and car park at Robin Hoods Bay Grid Ref. 950055 Leave towards village hall with toilets on your right	HALL TOILETS
0.21	0.21	Turn right onto tarmac road	
0.35	0.56	Continue ahead at crossroads and uphill with church on left hand corner	
0.54	1.1	Turn left on road signed to Fyling Hall and "unsuitable for long vehicles"	
0.07	1.17	Continue round to your right on track signed to Y.H.A and school	
0.12	1.29	Follow bridleway uphill through woods and then downhill on a wider track into another wood	
1.03	2.32	Downhill passing two houses and then uphill into wood	
0.09	2.41	Through gate and follow wire fence on your right	
0.23	2.64	Through gate and then back into woods on stony track that turns quite muddy when wet	
0.28	2.92	When out of the wood turn left on a track signed to Fylingthorpe Hall	
0.05	2.97	Through gate and follow the wall along the right hand side of a field	
0.23	3.2	Turn right at the end of the field through a gate following sign to Flyling Old Hall	

| | | LOCATION - ROBIN HOODS BAY AND RAVENSCAR | DISTANCE |
| 73% OFFROAD | | DIFFICULTY - EASY | 11.54 MILES |
SPLIT DISTANCE	TOTAL DISTANCE	DESCRIPTION BETWEEN POINTS	DIAGRAM OF LOCATION
0.28	3.48	Through gate and ahead	
0.25	3.73	Gate and pass farm on right	
0.08	3.81	Gate then onto tarmac	
0.31	4.12	Right at junction then follow track round to left and downhill	
0.24	4.36	Straight ahead at junction, ignore track on right	
0.05	4.41	Right onto bridleway opposite house then downhill through wood on narrow track	
0.15	4.56	Through gate and keep left downhill	
0.14	4.7	Cross river then left through gate, follow track uphill	
0.27	4.97	Through gate then uphill towards buildings	
0.15	5.12	Cross old railway line then through farmyard, keep left in front of two buildings. Turn right with barn on left then uphill to junction, turn left after gate.	
0.46	5.58	Ahead uphill at junction, ignore road on left.	
0.63	6.21	Left onto small track next to bridleway sign	

	LOCATION - ROBIN HOODS BAY AND RAVENSCAR		DISTANCE
73% OFFROAD	DIFFICULTY - EASY		11.54 MILES

SPLIT DISTANCE	TOTAL DISTANCE	DESCRIPTION BETWEEN POINTS	DIAGRAM OF LOCATION
0.43	6.64	Track widens, ignore track on left	
0.11	6.75	Onto tarmac	
0.37	7.12	Turn left and downhill to Ravenscar (or turn right to the tea-room at the top of the road)	
0.35	7.47	Turn left here at the National Trust coastal station	HOTEL
0.24	7.71	Bear left to join old railway track	
1.83	9.54	Cross tarmac road	
1.04	10.58	Cross tarmac road near cricket field	
0.71	11.29	Turn right onto tarmac	
0.03	11.32	Turn left signed to village hall	
0.22	11.54	End	CAR PARK

Route 10

Beggars Bridge, Lealholm and Glaisdale

Total Distance: 6.81 miles   **Offroad:** 52%

Start/Finish: Beggar's Bridge. Grid reference 784 055

Although this route may be short, do not be fooled into thinking it is a quick jolly! There are just a few hills in this one.

Park your car under or near the arch of the Railway Bridge adjacent to the narrow Beggar's Bridge. Set off by crossing the road bridge over the River Esk and follow the road left alongside the river. After about 250 metres you see a signfor "Limber Hill". Do not turn right uphill at this junction, but continue ahead still following the river. 200 metres further on you arrive at another junction. Continue ahead along a road marked with a dead end sign. Ride towards The Grange. Just before you come to the gate to the farm, go through the gate ahead of you into a grassy field.

Keep right uphill for about 200 metres to a fence ahead. Turn right and through another gate following a wire fence on your right. After 300 metres, pass through another gate and follow a small track, keeping left. Continue through a farmyard and turn left uphill on tarmac. Stay on this road for about 0.5 miles to a signed bridleway on your left, to Thorngill Farm. On the approach to the farm keep left, pass through a gate and then turn immediately right. Now look for a tree on your left. Follow the track around the tree then downhill through trees to a footbridge in the valley bottom. If you get to the valley bottom and cannot see the small wooden footbridge, you have probably gone too far to the right. If so, try turning left and follow the stream until you find the bridge. Look at the tulip sketch in the route guide at 1.51 miles, if you are still confused.

Once you find the bridge, cross it and continue straight ahead, uphill. Keep the hedge on your right and after 150 metres pass through two gates as you cross an old railway route. About 200 hundred metres further on, turn left onto tarmac in front of a house. Follow the tarmac road uphill to a gate. Go through the gate then through the gate that is immediately on your left, toward Hill House Farm. Do not go through the next gate to the farm but instead keep right. Follow the dry stone wall on your left keeping close to this wall then follow a steep path downhill for about 60 metres. Go through a small gate on your left which takes you to a tarmac road. Turn right, then go through a gate on your left onto a signed bridleway. Ride over the top ridge of a field and then downhill across a field. At the bottom pass through another gate and under a railway bridge to a farm. Go through a further gate then turn immediately right following a wooden sign with a fish carved on it.

Follow this track for 0.75 miles to a crossroads in Lealholm Village. You may wish to take a break here, so if you fancy a pot of tea and a snack continue ahead at the cross roads to find Shepherd's Hall team rooms about 200 metres away on your left. If you need something a bit stronger and fancy a swift pint cross the bridge to the Board Inn.

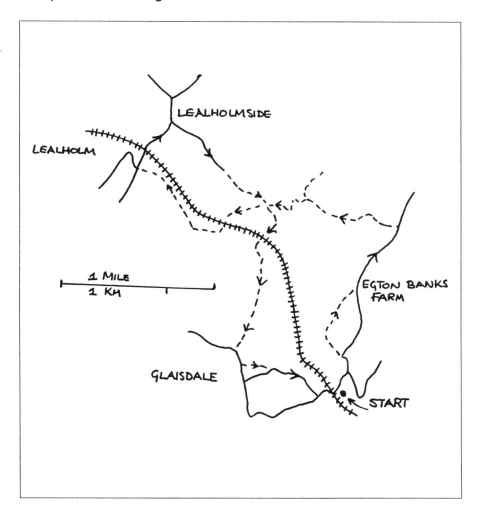

After you have had a break, you have a climb uphill passing the church. After 0.4 miles of uphill slog, turn right on a road adjacent to a post box. (Notice the memorial on the right to an American pilot who died in 1979 while ensuring his plane did not hit the village school). Continue along this road, going right where it forks after about 400 metres. 0.8 miles further on, pass through a gate onto a loose track at Park House Farm. Go downhill crossing over a railway bridge. Once you are on the level again, follow the grassy track keeping left all the time. After 300 metres you come to a footbridge on your right over the river. Cross the bridge and go steeply uphill to meet a tarmac road. Follow this road uphill for 0.5 miles to a crossroads and turn left towards Glaisdale. About 200 metres further on you will see the Robinson Institute (green railings) set back off the road on your left. Take the narrow path to the right of the building as it goes downhill. After 250 metres you join a tarmac road. Keep left going downhill to the valley bottom. Continue along the road for about 0.5 miles to a T-junction next to the Arncliffe Arms. Turn left downhill passing Beggars Bridge Tearooms as you arrive back to the car.

Try using this route in conjunction with Routes 5 or 11 (or even both) to give a longer ride.

		LOCATION - GLAISDALE AND LEALHOLM	DISTANCE
52% OFFROAD		DIFFICULTY - MEDIUM (SHORT BUT HILLY)	6.81 MILES
SPLIT DISTANCE	TOTAL DISTANCE	DESCRIPTION BETWEEN POINTS	DIAGRAM OF LOCATION
0	0	Start from under the railway bridge at Glaisdale Grid Ref. 784050 Cross river on road bridge and keep left following river on your left hand side	
0.13	0.13	Continue ahead at jucntion ignoring the very steep Limber Hill, keep the river on your left.	
0.15	0.28	Continue ahead on tarmac towards "The Grange"	
0.13	0.41	When the road turns left at a gate towards The Grange continue ahead through a gate into a field and uphill	
0.1	0.51	Turn right then through gate, keep fence on your left	
0.17	0.68	Gate then ahead on small track keeping left	
0.12	0.8	Pass through farmyarm and then turn left uphill	
0.29	1.09	Ignore road on left at the top of the hill	
0.19	1.28	Take signed bridleway on left to Thorngill Farm	
0.23	1.51	On approach to farm keep left through a gate and then turn right. Just after the gate look for a tree on your left & follow track around tree and downhill through trees. You should be following a small stream downhill to the valley bottom	
0.29	1.8	Follow track downhill to footbridge in valley bottom. Cross the footbridge and continue ahead uphill with hedge on your right	

		LOCATION - GLAISDALE AND LEALHOLM	DISTANCE
52% OFFROAD		DIFFICULTY - MEDIUM (SHORT BUT HILLY)	6.81 MILES
SPLIT DISTANCE	TOTAL DISTANCE	DESCRIPTION BETWEEN POINTS	DIAGRAM OF LOCATION
		NOTE - The track down from Thorngill Farm should be O.K. to find, however if you get to the valley bottom and there's no bridge turn left & follow the river to bridge	
0.1	1.9	Through a gate, cross the path of an old railway line and through a second gate.	
0.17	2.07	Turn left onto tarmac in front of house and follow track uphill	
0.22	2.29	At the top of the hill go through one gate then turn left through another gate towards Hill House Farm	
0.02	2.31	Do not go through the next gate to Hill House Farm but instead keep right with the stone wall on your left	
0.13	2.42	Keeping right of the wall follow a steep path downhill for 60 metres and then look for a small gate on your left. Go through gate onto tarmac	
0.02	2.44	Turn right onto tarmac and then left onto a signed bridleway across an open field	
0.24	2.68	Through gate and under railway bridge	
0.11	2.79	Pass Underpark Farm on left and go through gate Turn right following a sign with a carved fish	
0.73	3.52	Right at crossroads and uphill: For refreshments continue ahead at the crossroads to the Shepherds Hall Tea-room, or turn left for the Board Inn	
0.42	3.94	Towards the top of the hill turn right with a post box on your right. Notice the plaque on the stone near to the post box	P Box
0.21	4.15	Take right hand fork in the road	

		LOCATION - GLAISDALE AND LEALHOLM	DISTANCE
52% OFFROAD		DIFFICULTY - MEDIUM (SHORT BUT HILLY)	6.81 MILES
SPLIT DISTANCE	TOTAL DISTANCE	DESCRIPTION BETWEEN POINTS	DIAGRAM OF LOCATION
0.83	4.98	Pass through gate with Park House Farm on your left	
0.09	5.07	Cross railway bridge	
0.11	5.18	Keep straight ahead - do not go right to river	
0.09	5.27	Cross ford (or footbridge if you're a wimp) then follow track steeply uphill	
0.1	5.37	Join tarmac track and continue uphill	
0.55	5.92	Turn left towards Glaisdale village	
0.1	6.02	Just to the right of the Robinson Institute (the building with the green railings) take the narrow track downhill	
0.16	6.18	Join tarmac and bear right	
0.46	6.64	Turn left at junction opposite the Arncliffe Arms	
0.17	6.81	Pass Tearoom on left and back to start.	
		Try using this route in conjunction with routes 1 or 5 if you plan to do this linking of routes it's worth plotting them on your map first.	

Route 11

The Drovers' Road and Hawnby

Total Distance: 19.15 miles   **Offroad:** 82%

Start/Finish: Grid reference 475971 (Chequers Tearoom)

This is a good all-weather route along a drover's road and offers spectacular views on a clear day.

Start from Chequers Tearoom above Osmotherly. Set off on with the Tearoom on your left. After 0.7 miles, where the road turns left, go ahead and slightly uphill on a loose gravel track towards the trees of Crabtree Plantation. As you approach the wood on your right, pass through a gate and continue ahead.

Pass a bridleway that goes right into the woods and continue ahead as the track gets steeper, passing a stone cairn on your left. Follow the wide track as it levels out along the top of Black Hambleton. 1.17 miles after the cairn you come to a junction with a track off to your left. Do not take this track but follow the track around to the right that is signposted "Cleveland Way". After about 0.6 miles, pass through a gate. 0.5 miles later you come to a junction with a number of tracks. Bear right here, along a wide track signposted "Except for Access".

After about 1 mile, pass through a gate into North Woods, along a good fast track. Exit the wood through another gate and onto a rutted track (Hamilton Road). Stay on this track for 1.5 miles until you meet a tarmac road. Turn left onto the road signposted to Hawnby. After 0.4 miles, you come to a building on your right (Silver Hill Farm). Turn left here onto a signed bridleway around the left-hand side of a field. 0.4 miles from the old farm you come to a gate. Do not pass through it, but keep to the left of it following a wall on your right. After about 400 metres, pass through a gate and then continue ahead towards Sunny Bank Wood on your right.

Pass the wood on your right and you arrive at a junction with a number of tracks. Bear right and uphill towards a gate. Pass through the gate and follow a fence on your left. Go through two "double width" gates about 0.35 miles apart, then through a further gate and pass High Buildings on your left. About 400 metres after High Buildings, pass through a gate and keep left towards North Bank Wood. Follow the track downhill keeping the wood on your left. After 0.5 miles, you come to Sunnyside Farm. Keep right of the first building on the higher track. After 200 metres, turn a left hairpin bend at the second building, then continue along a farm track for 0.6 miles to a junction with a tarmac road.

Turn left towards Hawnby. After 300 metres you come to a junction with the Post Office on your left. Continue ahead uphill to a T-junction with a wooden shelter ahead of you. Go left here, passing (or going into) the Hawnby Hotel on your left. Continue downhill for about 600 metres to a junction. Go straight ahead here on a road marked "Unsuitable for Motors". Staying on the tarmac road, after 1.4 miles you will come to Arden Hall. Continue ahead uphill on the main track, passing through gates for 2.2 miles over the moor top to a junction with another wide track. (This is the point where you followed the "Except for Access" track). Go right here and retrace your tracks back to Chequers 4.1 miles away.

Chequers Tearoom is open every weekend, and on weekdays between April and October. To check times, telephone 01609-883291.

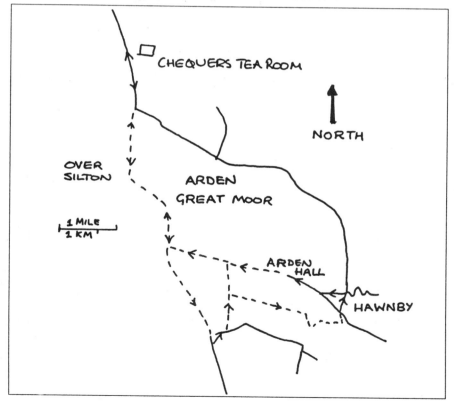

		LOCATION - THE DROVERS ROAD AND HAWNBY	DISTANCE
82% OFFROAD		DIFFICULTY - EASY	19.15 MILES

SPLIT DISTANCE	TOTAL DISTANCE	DESCRIPTION BETWEEN POINTS	DIAGRAM OF LOCATION
0	0	Starts from Chequers Tearoom (Grid Ref. 475971) With your back to the Tearoom turn left on tarmac	
0.7	0.7	When road turns sharp left continue ahead on loose track	
0.2	0.9	Through gate	
0.26	1.16	Pass wood on right ignoring the bridleway on your right into the wood	
0.58	1.74	Pass Cairn on less hand side	
1.17	2.91	Follow Cleveland Way sign towards Kepwick and Silton ignoring track on your left	
0.63	3.54	Through gate	
0.49	4.03	Bear right along a "Except for Access signed track	
1.03	5.06	Fast track through North Woods	
0.54	5.6	Out of woods and along a rutted track	
0.46	6.06	Stay ahead on main track at crossroads	
0.93	6.99	Left on tarmac signed to Hawnby.	

SPLIT DISTANCE	TOTAL DISTANCE	DESCRIPTION BETWEEN POINTS	DIAGRAM OF LOCATION
		LOCATION - THE DROVERS ROAD AND HAWNBY	DISTANCE
82% OFFROAD		DIFFICULTY - EASY	19.15 MILES
0.4	7.39	Left onto signed bridleway around the outside of the field	
0.41	7.8	Ignore gate and keep to left of the wall	
0.18	7.98	Through gate and straight ahead on grassy track towards Sunny Bank Wood on your right	
0.27	8.25	Keep right and slightly uphill and through gate then follow the fence on your left	
0.42	8.67	Through double width gate	
0.34	9.01	Through double width gate	
0.13	9.14	Through gate and pass buildings on your left	
0.22	9.36	Through gate and turn left towards North Bank Woods follow the track keeping wood on your left	
0.52	9.88	Keep right at Sunnyside Farm	
0.1	9.98	Hairpin left near to building	
0.6	10.58	Turn left onto tarmac towards Hawnby	
0.18	10.76	Pass post office on left and continue ahead uphill	

		LOCATION - THE DROVERS ROAD AND HAWNBY	DISTANCE
82% OFFROAD		DIFFICULTY - EASY	19.15 MILES
SPLIT DISTANCE	**TOTAL DISTANCE**	**DESCRIPTION BETWEEN POINTS**	**DIAGRAM OF LOCATION**
0.29	11.05	Turn left at the top of the hill by a timber shelter then pass the HAWNBY Hotel on your left	
0.35	11.4	Ahead on road signed "unsuitable for motors"	
0.65	12.05	Ignore bridleway sign and continue ahead	
0.8	12.85	Continue ahead and uphill at Arden Hall	
0.4	13.25	Still uphill ! And through gate	
0.95	14.2	Through gate at the top of the hill	
0.83	15.03	right and back to the track you came up on - follow the same route back to the start	
0.49	15.52	Through gate	
0.63	16.15	Bear left at Cleveland Way signpost, do not go ahead onto PRIVATE track	
1.15	17.3	Pass cairn then follow a good downhill with woods on your left. Ignore the bridleway sign after 0.58 miles	
0.84	18.14	Through gate	
0.18	18.32	Continue ahead on tarmac roads for 0.83 miles back to the Chequers tearoom after a total of 19.15 miles. Telephone number for Chequers is 01609 883291	

Route 12

Lealholm, Danby and Fryup

Total Distance: 13.73 miles   **Offroad:** 60%

Start/Finish: Grid reference 762076 (Lealholm)

Start from the car park near the public toilets in the centre of Lealholm. Turn right from the car park and travel uphill, following the signpost towards Whitby and Guisborough. After 0.53 miles you come to the top of the hill. Turn left here along a fairly level road, passing a Yorkshire Water Compound (surrounded by green wire fencing) on your right. About 0.4 miles further on, where the tarmac road turns sharp left, continue ahead on a gravel track signposted "unsuitable for motors". Turn left at a T-junction. Continue along this wide track for 1.7 miles until you join a tarmac road at Danby Beacon (the site of a Roman beacon). It is worth looking at the views from the trig point!

Go left and downhill on tarmac for 0.82 miles, to a stone pillar on your left, close to a junction. Turn right here along a signed bridleway. After 1.05 miles you come a wire fence with Clither Beck Farm ahead. Keep right here with the wire fence on your left. After 0.27 miles join the farm track and go straight ahead until you join a tarmac road. Turn left onto the road for about 200 metres and cross a bridge. Straight after this bridge turn left onto another signed bridleway, across Danby Low Moor, along Lord's Turnpike and towards Danby. When you come to a dry stone wall turn right and follow the track straight ahead for about 75 metres to a fork in the track. Go left here and downhill for 200 metres to a gate. Pass through the gate ahead, go downhill to the tarmac road, then right and downhill into Danby Village.

As you head towards the crossroads, you pass Stone House Bakery on your right. This tearoom is open Monday to Saturday from 9am to 5pm. However, out of summer months it is worth giving them a call to check opening times (Tel: 01287 660006).

Turn left at the Duke of Wellington and head downhill through the village. After about 0.25 miles, you pass a road on your left and then come to the Fire Station. Turn left here along Brook Lane towards the Fox and Hounds. After passing the pub on your left, continue uphill, and after passing the tennis courts take a signed bridleway that goes off on your right. Follow this track uphill to a gate. Continue uphill for about 0.8 miles passing two cairns on the way. After a 0.45 mile downhill you join a tarmac road. Cross this road at the T-junction going downhill with Slatehill House Farm on your left. After 0.3 miles, just after Stonebeck Gate Farm, turn left onto a bridleway and follow a track through gates for 0.75 miles. You then pass through two gates close together with Forrester's Lodge off on your left. Continue through two gates, after the second, keep left towards the bottom left corner of the field. After about 170 metres, pass through a gate following a stone wall on your left with a group of old trees on your right. About 0.22 miles further on go through another gate and head downhill to two stone pillars. Here, you will see Crag Farm on your left and a gate to your right, into Craig Wood.

Pass through the gate into Crag Wood (look out for the giant red toadstools). Pass out of the wood via another gate and continue ahead, uphill. About 0.24 miles further on, at the top of the hill, go to your right (see the sketch in the route card at 11.46 miles) and follow the farm track downhill for 400 metres to a tarmac road. Turn left onto tarmac and pass Furnace Farm on your right after about 0.25 miles (do not turn left here but continue ahead). After 0.46 miles, pass Wheatbank Farm on your left. Ignore the road on your right to Fryupdale. 100 metres further turn left on to an unsigned tarmac road.

After 0.41 miles you will pass Wild Slack Farm with a duck pond on your right. Pass over a cattle grid and turn left. Stay on this main road downhill back into Lealholm and back to the start again.

	LOCATION - LEALHOLM DANBY & FRYUP		DISTANCE
60% OFFROAD	DIFFICULTY - MEDIUM		13.73 MILES
SPLIT DISTANCE	TOTAL DISTANCE	DESCRIPTION BETWEEN POINTS	DIAGRAM OF LOCATION
0	0	Start from car park in the center of Lealholm Grid Ref. 762076 Turn right from car park, uphill signed Whitby	
0.53	0.53	Turn left at the top of the hill and pass a fenced Yorkshire Water compound with a green wire fence	
0.37	0.9	Straight ahead on stony track, unsuitable for motors	
0.28	1.18	Left at T junction following the main track	
1.71	2.89	Left onto tarmac at Danby Beacon and downhill	
0.82	3.71	Opposite stone pillar turn right onto a signed bridleway	
1.05	4.76	Keep right of Clither Beck Farm with fence on left	
0.27	5.03	Join farm track following tarmac road	
0.19	5.22	Left onto tarmac	
0.1	5.32	Cross bridge and bear left onto signed bridleway called the Lords Turnpike	
0.71	6.03	Right at gate in the wall and then straight ahead	
0.06	6.09	Keep left at farm and downhill	

		LOCATION - LEALHOLM DANBY & FRYUP	DISTANCE
60% OFFROAD		DIFFICULTY - MEDIUM	13.73 MILES
SPLIT DISTANCE	TOTAL DISTANCE	DESCRIPTION BETWEEN POINTS	DIAGRAM OF LOCATION
0.11	6.2	Through gate then downhill to road	
0.14	6.34	Turn right onto tarmac and then downhill towards Danby village	
0.15	6.49	Pass (or enter) Stonehouse Bakery tearoom and the Duke of Wellington public house and turn left at the crossroads. Tel 01287 660006 for tearoom	
0.23	6.72	Cross river bridge	
0.23	6.95	Ignore road on your left and then bear left near to the fire station onto Brook Lane passing the Fox and Hounds public house	
0.58	7.53	Pass tennis courts on both sides and then turn right onto a signed bridleway uphill	
0.17	7.7	Through gate onto moor	
0.37	8.07	Pass cairn on right	
0.34	8.41	Pass another cairn and take a look at the view for a few moments before a good downhill	
0.45	8.86	Onto tarmac and straight ahead downhill passing Slate Hill House farm on your left	
0.3	9.16	Turn left onto signed bridleway immediately after passing Stonebeck Gate Farm on your left stay on track passing through several gates	
0.76	9.92	Pass through two gates close together ignoring the track on your left to Foresters Lodge+D9	

SPLIT DISTANCE	TOTAL DISTANCE	DESCRIPTION BETWEEN POINTS	DIAGRAM OF LOCATION
	LOCATION - LEALHOLM DANBY & FRYUP		DISTANCE
60% OFFROAD	DIFFICULTY - MEDIUM		13.73 MILES
0.1	10.02	Through gate and follow track between two stone walls	
0.37	10.39	Through gatehole and bear left towards the bottom far corner of the field The important gateposts have waymarkers on them	
0.09	10.48	Through gate and then follow a wall on your left passing a group of old trees on your right	
0.22	10.7	Pass through gate	
0.14	10.84	Pass between two stone pillars and then look to your right, take the path through the gate into Crag Wood (Crag Farm on your left)	
0.13	10.97	Through gate and uphill through Crag Wood	
0.25	11.22	Through gate and out of wood	
0.24	11.46	At the top of the hill go to the single stone pillar and go right to pick up the farm track going downhill from Headhouse Farm to the road	
0.19	11.65	Turn left onto tarmac road	
0.23	11.88	Pass Furnace Farm on your right	
0.46	12.34	Pass Wheatbank Farm on your left ignoring the road on your right pointing to Fryupdale	
0.04	12.39	Left onto unsigned tarmac road	

LOCATION - LEALHOLM DANBY & FRYUP	DISTANCE
60% OFFROAD DIFFICULTY - MEDIUM	13.73 MILES

SPLIT DISTANCE	TOTAL DISTANCE	DESCRIPTION BETWEEN POINTS	DIAGRAM OF LOCATION
0.41	12.8	pass duckpond on your right and Wild Slack farm on your left	
0.24	13.04	Cross cattle grid and then turn left	
0.36	13.4	Ignore the road on right to Glaisdale	
0.33	13.73	Back to car park at the start	CAR PARK

Route 13

Ravenscar, Scalby and Harwood Dale

Total Distance: 19.26 miles   Offroad 67%

Start/Finish: Grid reference 981016 (Ravenscar)

This route follows the old railway line that runs from Whitby to Scarborough then across to Harwood Dale Forest. It returns via a moorland track to the beginning. This is recommended as a dry weather ride as the cross-country track gets very "squidgy" after a period of wet weather.

Park on the roadside near the toilets in Ravenscar, and set off with them on your right. After 50 metres follow the main road as it turns to the right (just by the entrance to the Raven Hall Hotel). Follow the road with the sea on your left for about 600 metres to Foxcliffe tearoom. Turn right in front of the tea-room and follow the track as it turns left to join the old railway line behind a house. Go over the stile and onto the railway line and, after half a mile pass under a road bridge.

A mile further, pass through two gates about 250 metres apart and pass Bee's Nest Farm on your right. Stay on the track through another gate before passing an old platform and buildings that have been converted into a house. Continue through gates and under bridges, passing the Hayburnwyke Hotel on your left. Cross the track leading to the Hotel, and go through another gate. Continue along the track for 2 miles going over one bridge then under another.

When you come to the tarmac road at Station House in Cloughton, turn right and then left, to pass Station House on your left. Join the railway line again through gates then under a bridge, and after one mile join the main road to Scarborough North Bay.

Cross the road, turn left for about 40 metres, then right through a gate back onto the old railway track again. After one mile, the railway track stops as you come to a housing estate. Turn left on to the tarmac road, and follow it to the T-junction at the end. Turn left along Field Close Road for 50 metres, then turn right at a T-junction onto Station Road. Follow this road past the tennis courts to some crossroads. Go ahead onto the high street crossing the Whitby-Scarborough road with care.

As you cross this busy road, you will be able to see Scalby Methodist Hall about 200 metres ahead. Pass three pubs on your left and the Yew Tree Cafe on your right. Stay on the high street passing a phone box on your right and continue downhill passing St Laurence's Church on the right. After passing the church go downhill, and turn right onto Carr Lane just after a post box but before a small bridge.

After 0.25 miles, when a track turns to the right, continue ahead uphill passing houses on your left. After a mile pass through a gate and ahead towards Prospect House Farm. Follow the signed bridleway in front of the farmhouse and through a gate. After 0.25 miles, go through another gate and across fields on a well-defined track. After a further half mile, you will see a house on your left (before Coomboots Farm). Go through two gates close together and pass to the right of the house, following the track up to the tarmac road.

Turn right onto the tarmac road and downhill for 700 metres to a crossroads. Go left here along Beacon Brow Road, passing a large modern house on your left. After 600 metres pass Beacon Farm on your right with the track now becoming quite grassy. About 600 metres further on there is a signed bridleway pointing across a field. Ignore this bridleway, and stay on the main track ahead, going down hill towards Silpho Brow Farm (you can see the farm ahead of you). The track now goes through two gates close together with the farm on your right. At this point the track turns to a tarmac road.

Follow this road for about 0.75 miles passing Surgate Brown Farm. At the 'T'-junction turn right and follow the fast tarmac road downhill into the valley bottom, ride up a short hill passing Thirley Cote Farm on your left and continue uphill on tarmac for 400 metres to a T-junction. Turn left, and follow a tarmac road for about 0.75 miles towards a sharp left-hand bend. About 50 metres before the bend take a signed bridleway on your right, and go along a wide track towards Harwood Dale Forest ahead of you. Once you reach the tree line, go through a gate and straight ahead into the wood. After about 300 metres you will meet a wide track. Turn left here and after only about 40 metres, take a smaller track on the right that goes slightly uphill.

Keep left after 200 metres over a small stream and follow the signed track. After 600 metres ignore the track on your right and continue ahead towards the farm building. Keep to the right of the house and join a wide track. Turn right as if you were going back into the wood again and, after 50 metres, follow the signed track on your left. Go through trees to join the Main Whitby to Scarborough road.

Turn left, then right on tarmac following the signpost to Ravenscar. After 650 metres ignore the tarmac road on your right and continue straight ahead. After 800 metres you see Moorland House on your left. Turn left along the wide track leading to it. Passing the house, continue ahead as the track narrows. Stay on this, sometimes boggy, track as it bends around to the right and eventually meets a tarmac road near a couple of houses (the house on your left is Smugglers Rock Tearoom — try the apple pie).

Go straight ahead at this junction, then downhill for over half a mile back to the Start.

		LOCATION - RAVENSCAR SCALBY & HARWOOD	DISTANCE
67% OFFROAD		DIFFICULTY - MEDIUM	19.26 MILES
SPLIT DISTANCE	TOTAL DISTANCE	DESCRIPTION BETWEEN POINTS	DIAGRAM OF LOCATION
0	0	Start from outside the toilets at Ravenscar at grid ref 981016 and go downhill towards the Ravenscar Hotel Turn right at the hotel gates following the main road	
0.41	0.41	Turn right in front of the Foxcliffe tea room and follow road for 100 metres to a stile next to the old railway	
0.08	0.49	Go over the stile next to the gate and onto the old railway line	
0.66	1.15	Under road bridge	
0.97	2.11	Through gate	
0.16	2.27	Through gate then pass Bees Nest Farm on your right	
0.61	2.88	Through gate near to house	
0.15	3.03	Pass old railway platform on your right and them go through a gate	
0.08	3.11	Under bridge	
0.52	3.63	Under bridge	
0.3	3.93	Pass Hayburn Wyke Hotel on your left	
0.13	4.06	Cross wide track then through gate	

		LOCATION - RAVENSCAR SCALBY & HARWOOD	DISTANCE
67% OFFROAD		DIFFICULTY - MEDIUM	19.26 MILES
SPLIT DISTANCE	TOTAL DISTANCE	DESCRIPTION BETWEEN POINTS	DIAGRAM OF LOCATION
1.03	5.09	Over bridge	
0.52	5.61	Under bridge	
0.44	6.05	Through gate and then turn right going around the front of Station House and back onto the railway track	
0.09	6.14	Through gate	
0.45	6.59	Through gate	
0.24	6.83	Through gate and under a bridge	
0.25	7.08	Through gate and cross the main road, turn left past a house then right through a gate back onto the railway track	
1.17	8.25	Turn left into a housing estate	
0.2	8.45	Left onto "Field Close Road"	
0.05	8.5	Right onto "Station Road"	
0.17	8.67	Pass tennis courts and cross main road at the cross roads onto "High Street" passing three pubs and the "Yew Tree" café (open Sundays!)	
0.28	8.95	Stay on High Street passing a phone box on your right and then downhill passing St Laurences Church	

		LOCATION - RAVENSCAR SCALBY & HARWOOD	DISTANCE
67% OFFROAD		DIFFICULTY - MEDIUM	19.26 MILES
SPLIT DISTANCE	TOTAL DISTANCE	DESCRIPTION BETWEEN POINTS	DIAGRAM OF LOCATION
0.1	9.05	After church, at the bottom of the hill turn right before a small bridge along Carr Lane	
0.22	9.27	Continue uphill passing houses on your left Note that Carr Lane can get pretty muddy after a period of rain.	
0.94	10.21	Through gate and then ignore the track on your right	
0.03	10.24	Follow signed bridleway on right, through a gate and in front of a house	
0.31	10.55	Through gate and across field on a well defined track	
0.43	10.98	Through "Double gate" system onto tarmac passing a house on your left	
0.05	11.03	Turn right downhill on tarmac	
0.33	11.36	Turn left onto Beacon Brow Road passing Beacon Cottage Farm on your left	
0.41	11.77	Pass Beacon Farm on your right and continue ahead on grassy track	
0.34	12.11	Ignore waymarked track on your left pointing uphill across a field and instead continue downhill towards Silpho Brow Farm	
0.29	12.4	Through gate	
0.07	12.47	Through gate onto tarmac passing farm on your right	

		LOCATION - RAVENSCAR SCALBY & HARWOOD	DISTANCE
67% OFFROAD		DIFFICULTY - MEDIUM	19.26 MILES
SPLIT DISTANCE	TOTAL DISTANCE	DESCRIPTION BETWEEN POINTS	DIAGRAM OF LOCATION
0.73	13.2	Pass farm on your right and turn right at a T junction onto a good tarmac downhill	
0.89	14.09	Uphill passing Thirley Cote Farm	
0.31	14.38	Uphill and turn left at the T junction	
0.77	15.15	100 meters before the sharp left hand bend in the road take the signed bridleway on your right	
0.44	15.59	Through gate and into a wood	
0.17	15.76	Left onto a wide track	
0.02	15.78	After 50 meters take the track on your right that goes slightly uphill. Do not go downhill towards the S bend	
0.11	15.89	Keep left over the stream following the waymarked track	
0.36	16.25	Ignore track on right and continue ahead towards a farm	
0.12	16.37	Keep right of the farm to a T junction, and turn right	
0.04	16.41	After about 75 metres turn left following a waymarked narrow track into the wood	
0.11	16.52	Take care and cross the main road and follow the Ravenscar sign	

		LOCATION - RAVENSCAR SCALBY & HARWOOD	DISTANCE
67% OFFROAD		DIFFICULTY - MEDIUM	19.26 MILES
SPLIT DISTANCE	TOTAL DISTANCE	DESCRIPTION BETWEEN POINTS	DIAGRAM OF LOCATION
0.15	16.67	Turn right towards Ravenscar	
0.34	17.11	Ignore road on your right	
0.44	17.55	Turn left onto track leading towards a house, pass the house and follow track as it sweeps round to the right	
1.01	18.56	Joint tarmac road next to the Smugglers Rock tearoom (try the apple pie)	
0.7	19.26	Downhill back to start	W.C

Route 14

Osmotherly, Scugdale and Carlton

Total Distance: 22.93 miles   **Offroad:** 67 %

Start/Finish: Grid reference 475971 (Chequers Tearoom)

Start from Chequers tearoom and head towards Osmotherly with the tea-room on your right. After 50 metres take the track on your right marked "Unsuitable for Motors". Follow this wide track for about 1.5 miles until it drops down to a ford. Cross the ford and go left onto a tarmac road towards Osmotherly, passing Cod Beck Reservoir on your left. As you approach the 30mph speed limit signs near Osmotherly, turn sharp right on to a gated road and uphill towards Swainstyle Farm. This uphill stretch is over a mile long but is not as bad as it looks! Pass through the gate at the bottom of the hill and continue uphill until the road turns sharp left. Just before the metal barriers on your right you will see two gates ahead. Go through the left-hand gate and along a wide bridleway.

After about 600 metres the bridleway arrives at Arncliffe Woods where you turn right. Go through a gate and take the track on the right that heads away from the wood. After about 0.76 miles bear right on the main track away from the stone wall. After approximately 250 metres, the track meets a tarmac road. Turn left and ride downhill for 400 metres. Immediately after you have passed over a cattle grid turn right and go through a small gate into Coalmore Wood. After about 200 metres turn left onto a wide track following the Cleveland Way sign.

After 500 metres you arrive at a viewpoint on your left. Take the left-hand track down a steep hill for 0.25 miles to a junction. Turn left and then right before the gate, following the Cleveland Way sign. Stay on this fast track through the wood for 0.7 miles, until you come to a Cleveland Way sign point-ing into a field (if you get up too much speed you could miss the signpost!). Follow this path over a stile and cross the field to a gate at the bottom. Pass through the ford and then turn left onto tarmac. Follow the tarmac road uphill past Hollin Hill Farm to a T-junction with a telephone box.

Turn right and follow the road for over 2 miles, as far as Scugdale Hall. Just before the wide gate, you will see a smaller gate on your left. Go through this and uphill onto a grassy track with the wire fence on your left. If you look up and to your right you will see a wire fence on the ridge — you should make for this point. When you get there, go through the gate and ahead towards the top of the ridge. Turn right onto a wider track and across the moor for about 350 metres. At a junction with three other tracks, turn left onto the wide track that you can see rising uphill a few hundred metres away. On your way towards the hill top (Carlton Bank) you pass Brian's Pond on your left and, after 0.6 miles, some crags on the right.

Continue ahead for another 0.6 miles (ignoring the track on your right towards the crags) until you see some huts on your right. Make for the large hut, just before you get to the hut, turn right onto a wide access track marked by white stones. Follow the access road downhill for 0.6 miles until you reach the road. Turn right along the road for 200 metres to Lord Stone Café on the left where you can have anything from a drink to a meal.

Leave the Lord Stone café by turning left out of the car park. After a short distance, the road starts to go downhill. This very fast downhill continues for about 2 miles. Just before the end of the downhill stretch, you will see a track off to your right marked as a footpath to High Crosslets Farm and Raisdale

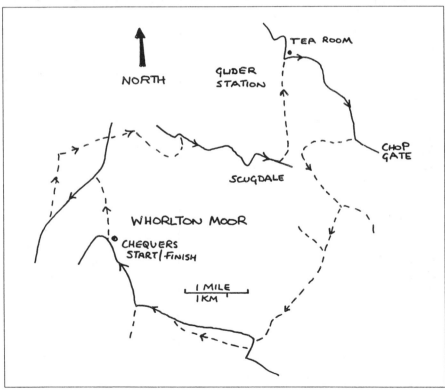

Mill. Take this track downhill and follow it left between buildings. After the last building on your right, take the signed bridleway uphill (Mill Lane). Follow the track through two gates and uphill on a narrower stony track with a house on your left. Follow the path with a stone wall on your left to join a wider track near to a green lane sign then uphill crossing over a forestry road. About 400 metres there is a track that goes off to your right, leading to Scugdale Hall. Ignore this track and continue uphill, keeping the wood on your left.

After one mile the track levels out on the top of Barker's Ridge. Follow the track as it bends to the right whilst ignoring a wide track on your left. At next junction you come to 0.84 miles further downhill continue ahead ignoring the track on the right. Another 0.5 miles further on, turn right at the T-junction and go downhill for 1.25 miles. Pass a small wood on your left as you continue to a gate. Pass through the first gate then ahead to a second with Rye Farm on the right. Pass through this gate, and continue ahead through a third to a T-junction at Hill End Farm. Turn right and downhill to another T-junction, go through a gate and turning left onto tarmac. Cross a ford, and 0.3 miles further on, join the Osmotherly to Hawnby road by Low Cote Farm.

Turn left, and go downhill following the Hawnby sign for about 400 metres to the bottom of the hill. Turn right through a gate onto a wide track, and after 100 metres, turn a tight left-hand hairpin and go through the second gate on your right. Follow the bridleway sign onto a well-defined track. Pass through another gate and across open moor with Waterfall Wood on your right. Follow the track downhill to cross Bawderis Beck passing through the gate ahead. Follow the beck for about 250 metres, then turn left following the dry stone wall uphill toward Dale House. Pass in front of the house and turn right before the outbuilding then through the gate. Take the wide track ahead going through two more gates for 0.8 miles. This brings you to the junction with a tarmac road. Turn left here and follow the road for 0.42 miles back to the start.

	LOCATION - SCUGDALE CARLTON & SNILESWORTH		DISTANCE
68% OFFROAD	DIFFICULTY - HARD BUT WORTH IT		22.93

SPLIT DISTANCE	TOTAL DISTANCE	DESCRIPTION BETWEEN POINTS	DIAGRAM OF LOCATION
0	0	Start from Chequers tearoom at Grid Ref 475971 Turn right towards Osmotherly on tarmac with tearoom on right.	
0.02	0.02	Take wide track on your right	
1.55	1.57	Cross ford and turn left onto tarmac and then pass Cod Beck reservoir on your left	
1.52	3.09	Just befoe the 30MPH speed signs turn sharp right and uphill through a gate towards Swainstyle Farm there is a B.T radio mast at the top of this hill	
0.97	4.06	Through gate	
0.15	4.21	Just before the metal road barriers go to your right and through the left hand gate of the two gates ahead of you	
0.31	4.52	When you come to a stone wall near to trees turn right and through a gate. After the gate keep right and across open moor	
0.72	5.53	Follow track as it curves right away from the stone wall	
0.16	5.39	Turn left onto tarmac and downhill	
0.19	5.58	Cross cattle grisd and then right through a gate into a wood	
0.1	5.68	Join a wide track keeping left and joinng the Cleveland Way route (signed)	
0.34	6.02	Bear left by a view point and follow Cleveland Way sign downhill	

		LOCATION - SCUGDALE CARLTON & SNILESWORTH	DISTANCE
68% OFFROAD		DIFFICULTY - HARD BUT WORTH IT	22.93
SPLIT DISTANCE	TOTAL DISTANCE	DESCRIPTION BETWEEN POINTS	DIAGRAM OF LOCATION
0.25	6.27	Turn left and then right before the gate, following the Cleveland Way sign	
0.69	6.96	Over stile and across field following the Cleveland Way sign	
0.19	7.15	Across field downhill to a gate and then cross a ford	
0.04	7.19	Turn left onto tarmac	
0.25	7.44	Pass Hollin Hill Farm and turn right onto tarmac near to a telephone box. Continue ahead passing a "No Through Road" sign	
1.98	9.42	Just before the gate to Scugdale Hall turn left and through a gate, follow the grassy path uphill	
0.09	9.51	Through gate and uphill. If you look up to the ridge slightly to the right you can see a gate, follow the track uphill making for this gate	
0.19	9.7	Through gate and follow track to the top of the ridge and then continue ahead on well defined track	
0.09	9.79	Turn right onto a wider track and then pass a small pond on your left (this may be dry in summer)	
0.22	10.01	Turn left at the junction with three other tracks Pass "Brians Pond" on your left and contine ahead following the track that goes uphill in the distance	
0.62	10.63	Pass some crags on your right	
0.39	11.02	When you see a large hut on your right head towards it and them turn right picking up a wide track that leads you downhill - Fast!	

		LOCATION - SCUGDALE CARLTON & SNILESWORTH	DISTANCE
68% OFFROAD		DIFFICULTY - HARD BUT WORTH IT	22.93

SPLIT DISTANCE	TOTAL DISTANCE	DESCRIPTION BETWEEN POINTS	DIAGRAM OF LOCATION
0.78	11.8	Continue downhill to met with a tarmac road , turn right at the bottom	
0.16	11.96	Turn left into car park of Lord Stone café for a well earned break - try the bacon & egg sandwiches	
0	11.96	Turn left after your break back onto tarmac road	
1.99	13.95	After a long downhill take the wide track on your right towards High Crosslets Farm and Raisdale Mill	
0.2	14.15	Follow track around to the left between buildings and then take the signed bridleway on your right after the last building	
0.45	14.6	Through two gates and follow the track uphill with a wall on your left	
0.14	14.74	Pass green lane sign and uphill on main track	
0.19	14.93	Cross a wide track and pass a wood on your left going uphill towards Bilsdale radio mast	
1.03	15.98	Ignore track on your left and follow main track with the radio mast slightly to your left	
0.84	16.82	Ignore track on your right	
0.54	17.36	Turn right at T junction	
0.59	17.95	Ignore track on your left	

	LOCATION - SCUGDALE CARLTON & SNILESWORTH		DISTANCE
68% OFFROAD	DIFFICULTY - HARD BUT WORTH IT		22.93

SPLIT DISTANCE	TOTAL DISTANCE	DESCRIPTION BETWEEN POINTS	DIAGRAM OF LOCATION
0.31	18.26	Small wood on left	
0.24	18.5	Through gate	
0.14	18.64	Gate and then Rye Farm on your right	
0.11	18.75	Through gate & right at T junction with Hill End Farm at T junction	
0.14	18.89	Downhill across field to T junction and turn left onto tarmac	
0.11	19	Ford that is often dry	
0.32	19.32	Join main road by postbox at Low Cote Farm Go downhill towards Hawnby	
0.25	19.57	Turn right and through gate onto track	
0.07	19.64	Take track through the second gate on your right following bridleway sign	
0.2	19.84	Through gate and follow signed track across the moor with Waterfall Wood below on your right	
0.69	20.53	Follow sign over the beck and then through a gate	
0.16	20.69	Follow beck for 250 metres then follow wall uphill towards Dale House	

		LOCATION - SCUGDALE CARLTON & SNILESWORTH	DISTANCE
68% OFFROAD		DIFFICULTY - HARD BUT WORTH IT	22.93

SPLIT DISTANCE	TOTAL DISTANCE	DESCRIPTION BETWEEN POINTS	DIAGRAM OF LOCATION
0.1	20.79	Pass in front of the house and turn right before the barn then continue through gate	
0.05	20.84	Ahead on track over open moor then through gate	
0.56	21.4	Through gate	
0.11	21.51	Turn left onto tarmac	
0.61	22.12	Ignore the track on your left and stay on the tarmac road back towards the start	
0.81	22.93	Back at Chequres tearoom	TEA ROOM

Route 15

Rosedale

Total Distance: 14.99 miles   **Offroad:** 62%

Start/Finish: Grid Reference 724959

This route is one of my favourites in the book. However, the hill at the start has to be the hardest test within this book. If you don't like steep hills, it's worth trying to get a lift to the top of Chimney Bank or, if there is a group of you riding, start from the top and leave a car at the bottom.

Start from Rosedale village centre, outside the Bakery tearoom and shop. Set off with the bakery tearoom on your left and the Abbey tearoom on your right. After about 100 metres turn right and up the very steep Rosedale Chimney Bank. On the way to the top of the bank, pass the White Horse pub on your left. Once at the summit and the road starts to level out.

Please note that the next mile or so of the route is on private land, and you are riding it thanks to the kind permission of the landowner. Please ride with consideration for both countryside and wildlife – this permission can be withdrawn by the landowner.

Take a track on your left that leads towards a small mound about half a mile away. This mound should have a stone cross (Ana Cross) which you can see from the road – if it hasn't been knocked over. Pass to the left of Ana Cross and continue on a wider track for about 300 metres until you come to a crossroads. Turn right here onto another wide track that can become quite muddy and sticky in the winter or after heavy rain.

After another 300 metres, the track you are on will merge with a path leading back to Ana Cross. Continue straight ahead and downhill for a further 1½ miles across Spaunton Moor until you reach a seat near the junction with some footpaths. Continue downhill through a gate and onto a tarmac road passing the Grange Hotel on your left.

At the bottom of the hill turn left at the T-junction and follow the main road out of Lastingham Village (or right for a drink at the Blacksmiths Arms). After three-quarters of a mile you cross a bridge on a curve in the road. a quarter of a mile later where the road takes a sharp right, take the uphill lane off to your left, ignore the signed footpath over the fence.

At the top of the lane cross a cattle grid and pass through a gate and continue ahead on a wide track. Where the track turns towards a house, continue ahead on a smaller track. After a further 600 metres where the wall on your

Ana Cross, on Spaunton Moor, after ascending Rosedale Chimney Bank

right ends, continue ahead over open moor. Stay on this track for another 2¼ miles where you pass Hollins Farm on your right. Turn left where the track that you are on joins the wider one. After about 150 metres pass through a gate and continue ahead for nearly a mile. Pass a house on your left and then in front of the White Horse pub (the one you passed going up the bank).

Take the tarmac road opposite the White Horse (do not go up or down the bank). After a quarter of a mile pass Low Farm on your left. A mile further on, keep right and around Crag View Cottage.

After 300 metres the tarmac road turns to a wide stony track. Pass through a gate and after 600 metres keep right ignoring the track on your left to Medds Farm. 400 metres further on, pass through a gate with some static caravans on the right. After another 400 metres, pass High House Farm on your left and go through the left-hand of the 2 gates ahead.

Pass a small wood on your left, continuing ahead until you come to two more gates side by side. This time take the right-hand gate and keep to the track on your right. Pass through two more gates about 200 metres apart, and ahead on Daleside Road. After half a mile, pass through a gate and follow the track

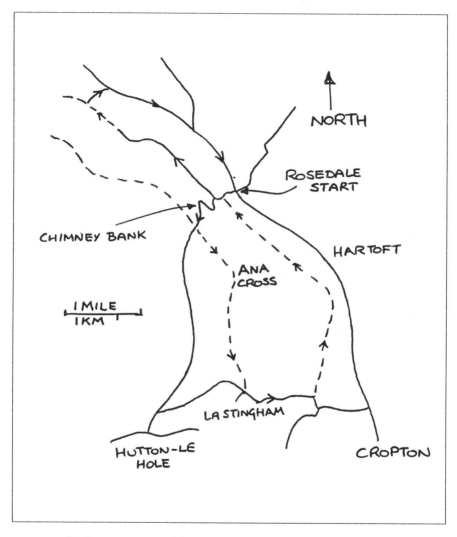

across to the far top corner of the field. Pass through another gate near Moorland Farm onto a tarmac road..

Turn right downhill on tarmac and cross the ford in the dip. Continue uphill to a T-junction and turn right. After 1¼ miles pass Hill Cottages and a phone box. Three-quarters of a mile further on, turn right at another T-junction and follow the road downhill back to the start in Rosedale Abbey.

		LOCATION - ROSEDALE	DISTANCE
61% OFFROAD		DIFFICULTY - MEDIUM WITH 1 STEEP CLIMB	14.99

SPLIT DISTANCE	TOTAL DISTANCE	DESCRIPTION BETWEEN POINTS	DIAGRAM OF LOCATION
0	0	Start from Rosedale village center from outside the Bakery Tea Room and shop Grid Ref 724959 Go south with the tearoom on your left	
0.07	0.07	Turn right up the very steep Rosedale Chimney Bank signed to the White Horse Hotel	
0.26	0.33	Pass the White Horse Hotel on the way up	
0.68	1.01	At the top of the bank turn left onto a wide track across the moor towards a small mound (Ana Cross). **Please note that you are now riding on private land**	
		so please ride with consideration for both the landowners property and the wildlife. Permission can be withdrawn at any time	
0.51	1.52	Pass to the left of Ana Cross staying on the wide track	
0.37	1.89	Turn right onto wide track	
0.32	2.21	Stay on wide sandy track as a track from Ana Cross merges from your right and continue downhill	
1.59	3.8	Pass viewpoint with a seat on your right and continue downhill	
0.09	3.89	Through gate and onto tarmac passing the Grange Hotel on your left	
0.24	4.13	Turn left at junction (or right to the Blacksmiths Arms)	
0.02	4.15	Follow main road through village	

		LOCATION - ROSEDALE	DISTANCE
61% OFFROAD		DIFFICULTY - MEDIUM WITH 1 STEEP CLIMB	14.99
SPLIT DISTANCE	TOTAL DISTANCE	DESCRIPTION BETWEEN POINTS	DIAGRAM OF LOCATION
0.82	4.97	Over bridge	
0.28	5.25	Left onto a wide lane uphill	
0.36	5.61	Over cattle grid and through gate following the track ahead	
0.33	5.94	When track turns right towards a house, continue ahead on a smaller track	
0.31	6.25	When the wall ends continue ahead on defined track over open moor	
1.04	7.29	Stay on main track	
0.42	7.71	Follow track as it goes steeper uphill	
0.78	8.49	Pass house on your right	
0.07	8.56	Turn left onto wide track	
0.08	8.64	Through gate	
0.15	8.79	Pass house	
0.77	9.56	Pass the White Horse Hotel on your left (Nice pint of Theaksons) Pass pub and continue ahead on a tarmac road towards Thorgill	

		LOCATION - ROSEDALE	DISTANCE
61% OFFROAD		DIFFICULTY - MEDIUM WITH 1 STEEP CLIMB	14.99
SPLIT DISTANCE	TOTAL DISTANCE	DESCRIPTION BETWEEN POINTS	DIAGRAM OF LOCATION
0.25	9.81	Pass Low Farm on your left	
1.01	10.82	Follow tarmac road around Crag View Cottage the road turns into a wide stony track after about 300 metres	
0.48	11.3	Through gate and turn right with Medds Farm on your left	
0.21	11.51	Pass static caravans on your right then ahead through gate	
0.22	11.72	Through the left hand gate near to the run down High House farm	
0.26	11.99	Pass a small wood then through the right hand gate ahead, keep right.	
0.12	12.11	Pass through two gate close together	
0.45	12.56	Through gate and follow the track to the top corner of the field	
0.13	12.69	Through gate and then right downhill on tarmac	
0.18	12.87	Cross ford (mostly dry) in dip and then uphill	
0.14	13.01	Right at T junction passing houses after another 1.25 miles	
1.98	14.99	Turn right and downhill. Follow road back to start in Rosedale	

Route 16

Hutton-le-Hole and Appleton-le-Moors

Total Distance: 10.75 miles   **Offroad:** 62%

Start/Finish: Grid Reference 724959

This is a fairly easy route and has a good variety of terrain with tarmac, open farmland and woods. The big challenge is to see if you can cross the ford near Appleton Mill Farm without getting your feet wet!

Set off from Lastingham village from the bottom of the road leading uphill to the Grange Hotel, opposite the telephone box. Turn right on the road through the village passing between the church and the Blacksmiths Arms. Continue out of the village and after about half a mile take a sharp right on the road signed to Hutton-le-Hole. After a further mile you pass a turning on your right to Rosedale and continue ahead for 600 metres to a T-junction. Turn left at the junction into Hutton-le-Hole village. If you feel the need for a break, try the Forge Tearoom; for opening times, phone 01751 417444.

Continue through the village with the river on your right. As you are about to leave Hutton-le-Hole, take the turning on your left just before the end of the speed limit sign. After 60 metres, take the wide grassy track up-hill signed 'Link Cropton 5 miles'. After 50 metres, the track splits in two. Keep right on the lower track and continue uphill. After 200 metres pass through a gate, then ahead between trees following a stony track.

After a further 200 metres ignore a track on your left and stay on the main track. Follow the track as it takes a sharp right turn and continues on Bottomfields Lane over open farmland. After 800 metres turn left, leaving the main track and continuing on a bridleway between two hedges. After 300 metres, ignore the footpath on your right and continue uphill into a small wood. After 500 metres go through a gate on your left. Keep left and follow a line of trees across a field, keeping Lingmoor Barn on your right. Go through the gate at the end of the field, and slightly uphill along a wide track called Lingmoor Lane.

After 600 metres you come to a crossroads with a footpath straight ahead. Turn right on a wide track called Ings Balk. About 1 mile along this track you come to a gate at another crossroads. Pass through the gate and continue straight ahead for half a mile to a junction with a tarmac road. Take a break here on the seat provided next to the gravestone of Catherine McDougall.

Turn left along the road for three-quarters of a mile following the road through

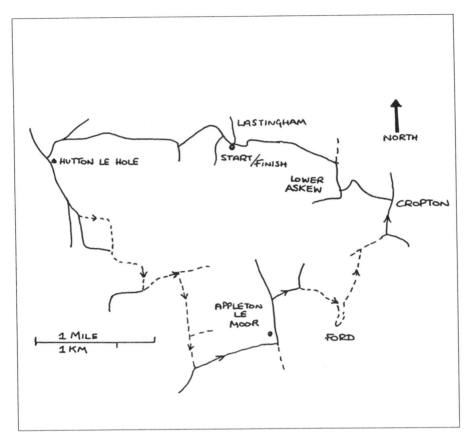

Appleton-le-Moors village passing (or calling into) the Moors Inn. Pass the church on your right and take the first right after you leave the village along Hamley Lane. After 600 metres where the road turns to the left, go straight ahead along a tarmac bridleway towards Appleton Mill Farm.

After a good downhill, pass between two farm buildings. Keeping to the right of the farmhouse on a track towards the trees of Mill Wood. After 200 metres you come to a ford mentioned near the beginning. Cross the ford — without getting wet! Once over the river, double back on yourself left and pass through two gates following a wide track uphill signed "Link Cropton". After 300 metres you see to a fork in the track. Take the left-hand track as it goes slightly uphill for a while and then downhill for 400 metres to two more gates. Turn right after the second gate following a 'Link Cropton' sign.

Barn Hotel and alternative tearoom

After 300 metres a track curves uphill on your right, ignore this and continue ahead on a level grassy track (Low Lane) for nearly a mile where it meets a road next to a bench.

Go left downhill then cross over Cropton Bridge. After the bridge, turn left passing Beckhouse Farm on your left. Half a mile further on, cross a bridge over the River Severn (What? The Severn bridge?). Ignore the road on your left to Appleton-le-Moor and keep right on tarmac for another 1¼ miles back to Lastingham.

		LOCATION - HUTTON-LE-HOLE & APPLETON	DISTANCE
41% OFFROAD		DIFFICULTY - EASY	10.75

SPLIT DISTANCE	TOTAL DISTANCE	DESCRIPTION BETWEEN POINTS	DIAGRAM OF LOCATION
0	0	Start in Lastingham village by the telephone box at the bottom of the road leading to the Grange Hotel	
0.06	0.06	Follow the main road around to your right between the church and the Blacksmiths Arms	
0.55	0.61	Take the signed road towards Hutton-le-Hole	
1.01	1.62	Continue on tarmac towards Hutton-le-Hole passing a turning on your right to Rosedale	
0.31	1.93	Left at junction into Hutton-le-Hole. Try the Forge tearoom on your left. For opening time ring 01751 417444	
0.32	2.25	Turn left just before the end of speed limit signs	
0.05	2.3	Follow a grassy track uphill signed "link - Cropton 5 miles"	
0.03	2.33	Keep right on lower track as it bends to the right and uphill	
0.09	2.42	Through gate on stony track between trees	
0.1	2.52	Ignore track on left	
0.33	2.85	Track turns sharp right then across open farm land on "Bottonfield Lane"	
0.4	3.25	Follow bridleway left between two hedges	

		LOCATION - HUTTON-LE-HOLE & APPLETON	DISTANCE
41% OFFROAD		DIFFICULTY - EASY	10.75

SPLIT DISTANCE	TOTAL DISTANCE	DESCRIPTION BETWEEN POINTS	DIAGRAM OF LOCATION
0.16	3.41	Ignore footpath on right and continue ahead uphill into a small wood	
0.27	3.68	Through gate and keep left. Follow the line of trees then through a gate at the end of the field keeping the farm on your right	
0.1	3.78	Through gate and continue on wide track (Lingmoor Lane) going slightly uphill	
0.35	4.13	Where footpath goes straight ahead turn right on wide track over open fields (ings balk)	
0.47	4.6	Footpath left and right - continue ahead on wide track to tarmac road	
0.44	5.04	Left on tarmac. Pass seat on your left just by the gravestone of Catherine McDougall 1890-1900	
0.76	5.8	Keep left onto Appleton-le-Moors main street ignore bridleway on your right Pass Moors Inn on your left	
0.36	6.16	1st right after you leave the village onto Hamley Lane	
0.31	6.47	Keep right at the millstone towards Appleton Mill Farm the track goes steeply downhill to the farm	
0.69	7.16	Through farmyard and keep to the right of the house on the track towards Mill Wood	
0.1	7.26	The Challenge ! Cross the ford without putting your feet down. After the ford double back left and through two gates following a wide track signed "Link Cropton"	
0.17	7.43	At the first fork in the track turn left . The track goes slightly uphill for a short distance and then downhill	

LOCATION - HUTTON-LE-HOLE & APPLETON			DISTANCE	
41% OFFROAD		DIFFICULTY - EASY	10.75	
SPLIT DISTANCE	TOTAL DISTANCE	DESCRIPTION BETWEEN POINTS	DIAGRAM OF LOCATION	
0.18	7.61	Downhill for 350 metres and through two gates. Turn right at the junction signed "Link Cropton"	
0.18	7.79	Keep left on narrower level grassy track (Low Lane)	
0.9	8.69	Left and downhill on tarmac	SEAT
0.17	8.86	Cross "Cropton Bridge" and then turn left passing Beckhouse Farm on your left	
0.54	9.4	Over bridge crossing the river Seven	
0.1	9.5	Keep right on road that takes you back to Lastingham Ignore the road to Appleton-le-Moors	
0.25	10.75	END	

Route 17

Gillamoor and Kirkbymoorside

Total Distance: 9.18 miles **Offroad:** 70%

Start/Finish: Grid Reference 683902 (Gillamoor)

Start from Gillamoor Main Street with your back to the Methodist church. Set off to your right towards the parish church and follow the road around to your left and down a fast tarmac downhill. At the end of the downhill straight as the road turns to the right, follow the bridleway to Faddell Rigg Farm. At the top of the hill keep left of the farmhouse along the main track. After about 200 metres, you pass a footpath off on your right (ignore it). After another 600 metres there is a track off on your right-hand side, again ignore this and continue ahead.

About 700 metres after the track on the right, go through a gate and along a narrower grassy path next to an open field on your right. 200 metres further, near two gates on the path, turn sharp left and uphill to a gate with a tarmac road on the other side of it. Turn left and uphill on the tarmac road for a quarter of a mile and where the main road turns to the right, carry on straight ahead on a long straight narrow road for 1 mile (signed to Gillamoor).

Turn left at the T-junction and then after 100 metres, turn right just before the pub. After just a few metres, the road curves around to the right. Continue straight ahead here on a tarmac track.

After three-quarters of a mile follow the signed bridleway track, with the golf course on your right-hand side. After a further half mile, turn right and through a wide gate passing High Park Farm on your right. Just after the farmhouse pass through a gate on your left-hand side and onto a well-defined track. After half a mile pass through another gate and keep left following a good grassy track. After half a mile through trees along Manor Vale, go through a gate and onto tarmac between houses and onto a junction with Park Lane. If you want a break for refreshments turn right here and go down into Kirkbymoorside town centre 400 metres away, where there are pubs and a couple of tearooms. Try the 'Thomas the Baker' tearoom, we were wet and muddy and they still welcomed us. Tel: 01751 432641 for opening times.

If you do not want to detour for a cuppa, turn left onto Park lane and uphill. After 200 metres go through a gate onto a wide tarmac track. 300 metres further on go through another gate and back onto a stony track. After another 400 metres go through yet another gate, back onto tarmac then straight ahead towards Low Park Farm.

After about 350 metres, cross a cattle grid and turn left back onto a wide track with woods to your right (Cockshot Plantation). After 100 metres ignore the track off on your right. Also ignore two more tracks close together on your right some 600 metres further on. About 200 metres after the two tracks on your right, the main track bends to the left. Just on the bend take the signed bridleway taking you into the wood (Rumsdale Plantation).

100 metres into the wood, ignore the track on your right and keep left and downhill. After another 200 metres, go straight ahead and downhill at a staggered crossroads. After a further 400 metres downhill you arrive at a T-junction at the bottom. Turn left at this junction onto a wide track. After about 100 metres there is a track on your right, ignore this and continue ahead on the wide track.

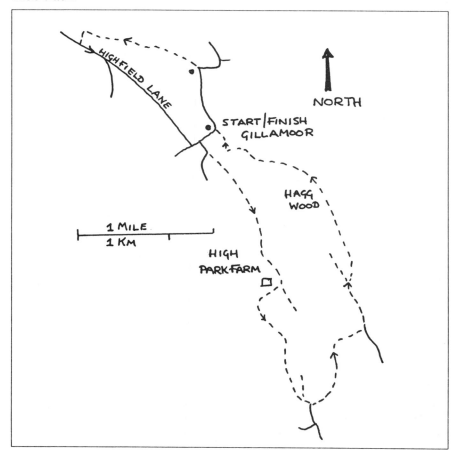

After 300 metres, you come to a 'sort of' crossroads. Keep right and go through a gate into open fields (this track is called Shepherds Road). After half a mile go through a gate and ahead into Hagg Wood, ignoring the track joining from your left. After travelling in the wood for a quarter of a mile, go through another gate and back onto open field, with the wood on your left.

After 200 metres yet another gate takes you up a steep track into the wood. At the top of the climb, take the track through the gate and cross the field to the far corner, where there are two gates. Dismount now as the bridleway turns into a footpath for the next 200 metres. Go through the right-hand gate and follow the footpath until it meets the tarmac road back at Gillamoor parish church. Turn left here and ride the last few metres back to the start.

Bridleway between Kirkby Moorside and Gillamoor, leading to Hagg Wood

LOCATION - GILLAMOOR AND KIRKBYMOORSIDE			DISTANCE
71% OFFROAD	DIFFICULTY - EASY 1 STEEP CLIMB		9.18 MILES
SPLIT DISTANCE	TOTAL DISTANCE	DESCRIPTION BETWEEN POINTS	DIAGRAM OF LOCATION
0	0	Start from gridref with back to Methodist church Go to your right towards parish church - follow road round to left and a fast Tarmac downhill	
		Don't overshoot the next junction	
0.57	0.57	Follow bridleway sign on wide track towards Faddel Rigg farm	
0.13	0.7	Keep to left of farmhouse	
0.1	0.8	Ignore footpath through gate on right	
0.32	1.12	Ahead at junction	
0.35	1.47	Through gate onto narrow grass track next to open field	
0.11	1.58	Follow bridleway sign uphill onto wider track Ignore the two gates	
0.07	1.65	Through gate and onto Tarmac uphill	
0.28	1.93	Follow narrow signed road to Gillamoor	
0.93	2.86	Left at T junction	
0.07	2.93	Turn right before pub	

| | | LOCATION - GILLAMOOR AND KIRKBYMOORSIDE | DISTANCE |
| 71% OFFROAD | | DIFFICULTY - EASY 1 STEEP CLIMB | 9.18 MILES |
SPLIT DISTANCE	TOTAL DISTANCE	DESCRIPTION BETWEEN POINTS	DIAGRAM OF LOCATION
0.05	2.98	Ahead on Tarmac track with houses on right	
0.7	3.68	Follow blue bridleway sign Pass golf course on right hand side	
0.55	4.23	Through gate to high park passing farm on right	
0.12	4.35	Through gate on left near to farm house	
0.48	4.83	Keep left at junction and follow good grassy track	
0.56	5.39	Through gate and along Tarmac road between houses until you meet "Park Lane"	
0.08	5.47	At junction with Park Lane turn right and downhill to Kirkbymoorside centre	
		If you don't want to detour into the town for a visit to a tea room or pub turn left onto Park Lane instead of right (This will mean the total mileage will not tie in properly)	
0.26	5.73	Phone number for "Thomas the Baker" tea room: 01751432641	TEA Room
		After the detour into town head back uphill and along Castlegate	
0.26	5.99	Keep right and uphill on Park Lane	
0.11	6.1	Through gate and onto wide track	

	LOCATION - GILLAMOOR AND KIRKBYMOORSIDE		DISTANCE
71% OFFROAD	DIFFICULTY - EASY 1 STEEP CLIMB		9.18 MILES

SPLIT DISTANCE	TOTAL DISTANCE	DESCRIPTION BETWEEN POINTS	DIAGRAM OF LOCATION
0.18	6.28	Through gate and onto stony track	
0.2	6.48	Onto Tarmac and ahead to Low Park Farm	
0.17	6.85	Over cattlegrid and left on wide track	
0.04	6.89	Keep left with wood on your right	
0.32	7.21	Ignore two tracks on right into wood	
0.07	7.28	Follow bridleway sign into wood and downhill until you meet "Park Lane"	
0.05	7.33	Keep left and downhill	
0.09	7.42	Continue downhill on steep track crossing wide track	
0.2	7.62	Keep to left at bottom of the hill	
0.06	7.68	Ignore junction on right and continue ahead	
0.15	7.83	Keep right and through gate into open field	
0.46	8.29	Through gate and into wood Ignore track joining on left	

		LOCATION - GILLAMOOR AND KIRKBYMOORSIDE	DISTANCE
71% OFFROAD		DIFFICULTY - EASY 1 STEEP CLIMB	9.18 MILES
SPLIT DISTANCE	TOTAL DISTANCE	DESCRIPTION BETWEEN POINTS	DIAGRAM OF LOCATION
0.23	8.42	Through gate and into field	
0.11	8.53	Left and through gate uphill into woods	
0.25	8.78	Out of wood and through gate into field Cross to far corner of field	
0.11	8.89	In far corner of field you come to two gates Go through the right hand gate and onto a footpath	
		You must now either carry or push your bike for the 250 yards of the footpath	
0.39	9.18	Join with the Tarmac road back at the parish church	

Route 18

Kildale, Rudland Rigg and Gillamoor

Total Distance: 31.86 miles   **Offroad:** 68%

Start/Finish: Grid reference 607094 (Kildale)

This route is the longest and possibly hardest of this guide, however it commands some of the best views. To make the most of this route I would suggest a fine day as it can get quite bleak on the top of Rudland Rigg in bad weather.

Start from the tearoom near Kildale railway station. Park in the car park at the Kildale railway station and turn right out of the car park. Once you come to the tearoom reset your trip computer to zero as the mileage readings start here.

Pass the tearoom on your left left to join the main road through Kildale village. Turn right along the main road for about 300 metres to a road on your left marked with a Cleveland Way sign and a Baysdale Farm sign. Take this road uphill for 600 metres and over a cattle grid. After a steep climb the road levels out and follows the ridge. Cross another cattle grid a mile after the first and continue ahead for half a mile until the road turns sharp left. At this corner take the track through two gates close together. Follow the track slightly uphill onto open moor.

After about 0.7 miles ignore a track on your left and continue ahead. A further 0.86 miles on you come to a junction with a wide track. Turn left here following the route of the Cleveland Way. Stay on this main track to Bloworth Crossing 2.5 miles away, ignoring two tracks on your left and a metal gate on your right. Bloworth Crossing is identified by a crossroads with a gate on your left.

Continue straight ahead at Bloworth Crossing passing first a gated track on your right after 0.5 miles and then a large stone (common stone) on your left 0.5 miles further on. Stay on this track for another 3.4 miles where you pass a trig point (Golden Heights) on your right.

The track now heads downhill for 1.8 miles of freewheeling where it meets a tarmac road. Continue straight ahead at this junction (do not turn right) crossing a cattle grid after 0.25 miles and straight ahead at Hope Inn Farm 0.4 miles further on. Follow the road to the top of the hill and where the main road turns right go straight ahead on the narrower road downhill signed to Gillamoor.

Turn left at the T-junction at the end of the narrow road following the main road through Gillamoor village and ignoring a road off to the right. Pass the church on your right and then downhill for over 0.5 miles to a junction signposted to Farndale. Turn left uphill along the Farndale road for nearly a mile where you turn right onto a wide bridleway. The wide track follows downhill for over 0.5 miles and through a gate into a farmyard (Park Farm). Keeping left of the farm, pass through a gate then ahead until you come to an open gate hole. Do not go through the gate but turn left on a path keeping the stone wall on your right. This easy to follow track continues alongside the wall through bracken until it comes to a further gate. After going through the gate the track descends to Cross Farm. Go straight ahead up a wide stony track for

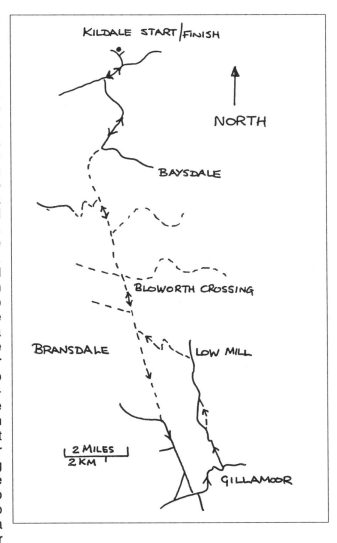

about 200 metres where it meets a road. Turn right and follow the road for 1.1 miles as it goes downhill back to a small car park with toilets at Low Mill.

Pass the car park and continue uphill until, after about 0.25 miles, you will see a sign pointing to the left marked "Bridleway to Rudland Rigg". Turn onto this bridleway towards a house (Horn End). When you reach the house go straight ahead on a grassy track through a gate. Follow this track through

Rudland Rigg, towards Gillamoor

another gate with a wire fence on your left. The track goes through more gates and passes an old farm building on your left (High Barn). Soon after passing High Barn go through one gate and towards another. Do not go through this second gate but follow the Yellow and Blue waymark sign left and around the outside of the dry stone wall.

Go through another gate then over the wooden bridge that crosses the River Dove. Follow the track as it heads uphill towards the ridge ahead. Keep left by the stone wall until you come to a gate in it. Pass through the gate and follow the path uphill (keeping to the right of the two trees ahead). The path curves to the right as it continues uphill and meets a small grass track. Go right still uphill through bracken. Go through yet another gate with a waymark sign and follow the track as it steepens through the bracken. The track soon levels off on a small path over heather and follows the side of the valley parallel with the ridge. Start to go slightly uphill, passing grouse butts until you join a wide, stony track on the top of the ridge.

Turn right here onto Rudland Rigg and retrace your tracks back to Bloworth Crossing (Crossroads with the gate on your right). Ride downhill for another 2.5 miles back to the Cleveland way sign. Leaving the wide track, turn right and uphill onto the narrower track that you rode down earlier. Follow this track back towards the road above Baysdale 1.5 miles away. Go back through the two gates and continue straight ahead onto the tarmac road (do not turn right) Follow the road along the ridge then downhill crossing two cattle grids to the T-junction at the bottom of the hill. Turn right here and follow the main road back to Kildale and the tearoom.

	LOCATION - KILDALE AND RUDLAND RIGG	DISTANCE
68% OFFROAD	DIFFICULTY - DIFFICULT-LONG CLIMBS	31.86 MILES

SPLIT DISTANCE	TOTAL DISTANCE	DESCRIPTION BETWEEN POINTS	DIAGRAM OF LOCATION
		Start from tea room in Kildale Parking is available near to the railway station ride back from the railway station to the tearoom	
0	0	Exit the tea room turning left towards Kildale village	
0.02	0.02	Turn right at junction in Kildale village	
0.28	0.3	Take road on left heading uphill towards Baysdale	
0.35	0.65	Gate over cattlegrid	
1.1	1.75	Gate over cattlegrid	
0.5	2.25	On top of ridge where road turns sharp left go ahead through two gates and onto open moor uphill	
0.69	2.94	Ignore track on left	
0.8	3.74	Join wider track Turn left onto Cleveland Way	
0.4	4.14	Ignore track on left	
0.86	5	Ignore bridleway on the left	
0.44	5.44	Pass metal gate on right	

LOCATION - KILDALE AND RUDLAND RIGG				DISTANCE
68% OFFROAD		DIFFICULTY - DIFFICULT-LONG CLIMBS		31.86 MILES
SPLIT DISTANCE	TOTAL DISTANCE	DESCRIPTION BETWEEN POINTS		DIAGRAM OF LOCATION
0.81	6.25	Continue straight ahead at Bloworth crossing		
0.15	6.4	Ignore gated track on right Bloworth plantation on right in valley		
0.55	6.95	Ignore track on right		
0.5	7.45	Pass large stone on left (Common Stone)		
0.15	7.6	Ignore track on left		
0.9	8.5	Ignore grassy tracks on right and left		
0.9	9.4	Straight ahead at crossroads		
1.44	10.84	Pass Trig Point (Golden Heights) on right		
1.33	12.17			
0.51	12.68	Straight ahead onto Tarmac		
0.24	12.92			
0.41	13.33	Pass Hope Inn Farm on right		

		LOCATION - KILDALE AND RUDLAND RIGG	DISTANCE
68% OFFROAD		DIFFICULTY - DIFFICULT-LONG CLIMBS	31.86 MILES
SPLIT DISTANCE	TOTAL DISTANCE	DESCRIPTION BETWEEN POINTS	DIAGRAM OF LOCATION
0.52	13.85	Uphill passing bridleway on left	
0.28	14.13	Follow narrow signed road to Gillamoor	
0.93	15.06	Left at T junction	
0.07	15.13	Pass Oak Tree pub on right	
0.27	15.4	Keep left of church and follow road on fast downhill	
0.67	16.07	Take road on left towards Farndale	
0.92	16.99	Turn right onto bridleway	
0.63	17.62	Keep left of farm	
0.07	17.69	Keep left of open gate and follow track through bracken following stone wall	
0.3	17.99	Through gate and downhill	
0.13	18.12	Straight ahead at farm on wide stony track that goes uphill	
0.14	18.26	Turn right onto Tarmac road	

	LOCATION - KILDALE AND RUDLAND RIGG		DISTANCE
68% OFFROAD	DIFFICULTY - DIFFICULT-LONG CLIMBS		31.86 MILES

SPLIT DISTANCE	TOTAL DISTANCE	DESCRIPTION BETWEEN POINTS	DIAGRAM OF LOCATION
1.01	19.27	Follow road to Low Mill car park	
0.06	19.33	Pass toilets and car park and continue uphill	
0.25	19.58	Take left onto bridleway signed to Rudland Rigg	
0.32	19.9	Ahead through gate onto grass track with house on left	
0.19	20.09	Follow track by wire fence through three gates	
0.26	20.35	Farm building on left	
0.06	20.41	Follow sign through gate and round outside of stone wall Do not go through second gate - keep left	
0.06	20.47	Through gate and left over small stream Go straight ahead towards the ridge ahead. Keep stone wall to your left until you come to a gate on your left	
0.1	20.57	Through gate and follow track uphill keeping to right of two trees ahead	
0.13	20.7	Follow track as it turns to right on smaller grass track uphill through bracken	
0.07	20.77	Through gate and uphill following signed track	
		Follow level track that runs parallel to Rudland Ridge	

	LOCATION - KILDALE AND RUDLAND RIGG	DISTANCE
68% OFFROAD	DIFFICULTY - DIFFICULT-LONG CLIMBS	31.86 MILES

SPLIT DISTANCE	TOTAL DISTANCE	DESCRIPTION BETWEEN POINTS	DIAGRAM OF LOCATION
0.85	21.62	Pass to the right of some shooting butts	
0.35	21.97	Turn right onto Rudland Rigg	
0.47	22.44	Ahead at crossroads	
0.9	23.34	Ahead at crossroads	
0.9	24.24	Ignore track on right	
0.15	24.39	Pass "Common Stone" again	
0.5	24.89	Ignore track on left	
0.55	25.44	Pass gated track on left	
0.15	25.59	Continue ahead at Bloworth crossing	
0.81	26.4	Ignore gate on left	
0.44	26.84	Ignore bridleway on right	
0.86	27.7	Ignore track on right	

LOCATION - KILDALE AND RUDLAND RIGG				DISTANCE
68% OFFROAD		DIFFICULTY - DIFFICULT-LONG CLIMBS		31.86 MILES
SPLIT DISTANCE	TOTAL DISTANCE	DESCRIPTION BETWEEN POINTS		DIAGRAM OF LOCATION
0.4	28.1	Track smaller track on right following Cleveland Way sign		
0.8	28.9	Ignore track on right		
0.69	29.59	Through two gates onto Tarmac and continue straight ahead		
0.5	30.09	Cross cattlegrid		
1.1	31.19	Cross cattlegrid		
0.37	31.56	Right at junction towards Kildale		
0.28	31.84	Left at junction towards tea room		
0.02	31.86	End		

Route 19

Glaisdale and Fryupdale

Total Distance: 16.06 miles   **Offroad:** 52%

Start/Finish: Grid reference 774055 (The Mitre Tavern, Glaisdale)

This route is a good one for any time of the year with a mixture of firm tracks, tarmac and narrow bridleway. The Shepherds Hall tearoom is also suitably located about two thirds of the way round.

Park your car near the Robinson Institute uphill from the Mitre Tavern. Set off by turning right and uphill with your back to the Robinson Institute. After about 600 metres take the signed bridleway on the left opposite High Leas farm. After 400 metres pass through a gate onto open moor on a grassy track. 600 metres further on turn right onto a wider more defined track and 30 metres afterwards keep right at a crossroads (do not follow the signed bridleway straight ahead).

Continue on this wide main track as it goes gently uphill, crossing Glaisdale Low Moor for about 1½ miles. There you join a tarmac road, ignoring a number of signed and unsigned footpaths and bridleways along the way.

Turn left onto the road and uphill for 1 mile where you come to some metal gates on your right. Go through the gate on the left, then keep left onto a signed bridleway (Cut Road). Stay on this easy to follow track crossing Glaisdale High Moor. After 0.66 miles, you pass a bridleway sign on your right pointing straight ahead. 0.44 miles further on you pass a second bridleway sign near a small stream.

Continue ahead for a quarter of a mile to a pile of stones on your right. 100 metres further on there is a second pile of stones near a bridleway on your left. Ignore the bridleway and look across slightly to your right to a stone building (Trough House). Continue ahead on the same track for a mile, passing Trough House and joining a tarmac road through a gate.

Turn right onto the road and follow it for 2½ miles as it goes downhill, gently at first but then getting much steeper. When you come to the junction at the bottom of the hill you will see Slate Hill House farm ahead of you. Turn right here and after 0.3 miles, (immediately after Stonebeck Gate Farm), turn left onto a bridleway following it for 0.75 miles. You now pass through two gates close together with Forrester's Lodge on your left. Continue ahead through two more gates, after the second, keep left towards the bottom left corner of the field. After another 170 metres, pass through a gate and follow a stone wall on your left with a group of old trees on your right. a quarter of a mile further on go through another gate and head downhill to two stone pillars. Here, you will see Crag Farm on your left and a gate to your right that leads into Crag Wood.

Pass through the gate into Crag Wood (spot the giant red toadstools). Pass out of the wood via another gate and continue ahead, uphill. About 0.24 miles further on, at the top of the hill, go to your right (see the sketch in the route card at 11.46 miles) and follow the farm track downhill for 400 metres to a tarmac road. Turn left onto tarmac and pass Furnace Farm on your right after about 0.25 miles (do not turn left here but continue ahead) After a further 0.46 miles, pass Wheatbank Farm on your left. Ignore the road on your right to Fryupdale. After 100 metres, turn left on to an unsigned tarmac road.

After 0.41 miles you will pass Wild Slack Farm with a duck pond on your right. Pass over a cattle grid and turn left. Stay on this main road downhill back into Lealholm You may wish to take a break here, so if you fancy a pot of tea and a snack cross the bridge and turn left at the cross roads to find Shepherd's Hall team rooms about 200 metres away on your left. If you need something a bit stronger and fancy a swift pint, try the Board Inn just before you cross the bridge.

After you have had a break, you have to climb uphill passing the church. After 0.4 miles of uphill slog, turn right on a road adjacent to a post box. (Notice the memorial on the right to an American pilot who died in 1979 while ensuring his plane did not hit the village school). Continue along this road, going right where it forks after about a quarter of a mile. A further 0.8 miles on, pass through a gate onto a loose track at Park House Farm. Go downhill crossing over a railway bridge. Once you are on the level again, follow the grassy track keeping left all the time. After 300 metres you come to a footbridge on your right over the river. Cross the bridge and go steeply uphill to meet a tarmac road. Follow this road uphill for 0.5 miles to a crossroads and turn left towards Glaisdale. About 200 metres further on you will see the Robinson Institute on your left and the end of the ride.

	LOCATION - GLAISDALE AND FRYUP		DISTANCE
52% OFFROAD	DIFFICULTY - MEDIUM		16.06 MILES
SPLIT DISTANCE	TOTAL DISTANCE	DESCRIPTION BETWEEN POINTS	DIAGRAM OF LOCATION
0	0	Start outside the Robinson Institute in Glaisdale (uphill from the Mitre Tavern, Grid reference 774055) and head uphill (turn right with your back to the institute)	
0.41	0.41	Left onto wide signed bridleway opposite "High Leas"	
0.19	0.6	Through gate and onto open moor	
0.42	1.02	Onto a wider more defined track	
0.04	1.08	Keep right - ignore bridleway sign pointing straight ahead	
0.34	1.42	Pass bridleway sign - continue ahead	
0.02	1.46	Ignore track crossing	
0.11	1.57	Ignore track joining from the right	
0.12	1.69	Ignore grassy track joining from right	
0.2	1.89	Ignore wide grassy track that joins from left	
0.14	2.03	Stay on main track	
0. 09	2.12	Ignore narrow signed tracks on right and left - straight ahead uphill to meet Tarmac	

		LOCATION - GLAISDALE AND FRYUP	DISTANCE
52% OFFROAD		DIFFICULTY - MEDIUM	16.06 MILES
SPLIT DISTANCE	TOTAL DISTANCE	DESCRIPTION BETWEEN POINTS	DIAGRAM OF LOCATION
0.32	2.44	Ignore signed bridleway on left and right	
0.34	2.78	Bear left onto Tarmac road	
0.42	3.2	Track joins road from right with bridleway on left Continue ahead	
0.55	3.75	Gates on right hand side Go through left hand gate and keep on left hand track	
0.66	4.41	Pass pile of stones and bridleway sign	
0.44	4.85	Pass wooden bridleway sign and cross small stream	
0.2	5.05	Pass stones and path on right	
0.06	5.11	Pile of stones marks bridleway to Rosedale Continue ahead towards Trough House (buildings ahead on the ridge)	
0.79	5.9	Pass Trough House on your right	
0.23	6.13	Through gate and right onto Tarmac	
0.97	7.1	Ahead ignoring bridleway on left and right	
0.13	7.23	Ignore bridleway on right	

LOCATION - GLAISDALE AND FRYUP			DISTANCE	
52% OFFROAD		DIFFICULTY - MEDIUM	16.06 MILES	
SPLIT DISTANCE	TOTAL DISTANCE	DESCRIPTION BETWEEN POINTS	DIAGRAM OF LOCATION	
0.65	7.88	Ignore bridleway	
0.83	8.71	Turn right at junction with road at Slate Hill House Farm	
0.29	9	Turn left on bridleway immediately after house (Stonebeck Gate Farm) and pass through several gates	
0.76	9.76	Through two gates passing Forester's Lodge on left	
0.1	9.86	Gate and onto track between walls	
0.37	10.23	Through open gatehole Keep left towards bottom left corner of field	
0.09	10.32	Gate then follow wall on left - group of old trees on right	
0.22	10.54	Gate	
0.14	10.68	Between two stone pillars and look towards your right Go through gate into Crag Wood	
0.13	10.81	Gate and continue through Crag Wood	
0.25	11.06	Gate and out of wood and ahead uphill	
0.24	11.3	At top of hill go to single stone pillar - go right onto loose Tarmac track Follow track downhill to junction	

		LOCATION - GLAISDALE AND FRYUP	DISTANCE
52% OFFROAD		DIFFICULTY - MEDIUM	16.06 MILES
SPLIT DISTANCE	TOTAL DISTANCE	DESCRIPTION BETWEEN POINTS	DIAGRAM OF LOCATION
0.19	11.49	Turn left	
0.23	11.72	Pass Furnace Farm	
0.46	12.18	Pass Wheatbank Farm ignoring road on right to Fryupdale	
0.04	12.22	Turn left on unsigned road	
0.41	12.63	Pass duck pond and Wild Slack Farm	
0.24	12.87	Over cattlegrid and turn left	
0.36	13.23	Ignore Glaisdale road	
0.33	13.56	Downhill into Lealholm village and over bridge (pub on left before bridge)	
		*The route continues ahead uphill - however you may want to turn left over the bridge to Shepherds Hall tea room	
0.42	13.98	Uphill to road on right with post box on corner	
0.21	14.19	Take right hand fork	
0.83	15.02	Pass Park House Farm and through gate	

LOCATION - GLAISDALE AND FRYUP			DISTANCE	
52% OFFROAD		DIFFICULTY - MEDIUM	16.06 MILES	
SPLIT DISTANCE	TOTAL DISTANCE	DESCRIPTION BETWEEN POINTS	DIAGRAM OF LOCATION	
0.09	15.11	Cross over railway bridge	
0.11	15.22	Continue straight ahead keeping the river on your right	
0.09	15.31	Cross the ford across the river (or use the bridge if you are a wimp) and follow the steep track uphill	
0.1	15.41	Join tarmac road	
0.55	15.96	Turn left at junction towards Glaisdale	
0.1	16.06	Finish back at the Robinson Institute	

Route 20

Newtondale

Total Distance: 6.06 miles   **Offroad:** 80%

Start/Finish: Grid reference 813906 (The White Swan, Newton-on-Rawcliff)

Although you can ride this route at anytime, a few of the tracks can get quite muddy during wet weather. Park your car in Newton-on-Rawcliff outside the White Swan. Set off by turning right, slightly uphill, with your back to the pub. After 200 metres, there are two tracks on your right. Take the wide, signed bridleway on the right marked "Link Levisham 4 miles".

After a quarter of a mile pass a footpath on your right then turn sharp left and downhill on a narrow signed bridleway. After 200 metres ignore a path on your right and continue downhill to a gate. Go though the gate and cross a field following a stone wall on your left. Go through another gate and bear right downhill, after a quarter of a mile pass through another gate, over a small steam then downhill to meet a road.

Turn right and downhill on the forest drive for half a mile to Levisham station. Cross the lines and take a break at the station. There is a drinks machine and toilets for your convenience. On Sundays in August, there are band concerts in the station paddock with a refreshment kiosk.

After your brief visit to the station go back to the road, turn right and cross the cattle grid. Follow the road for 0.6 miles as it heads steeply uphill doubling back on itself. Before the top of the hill, take the signed bridleway on your right, keeping to the left of the gate.

Follow the well-defined track for half a mile and pass through a gate then turn right and downhill into a wood. Pass through a gate after a quarter of a mile into a field next to the railway line. Pass through a second gate a quarter of a mile further on and take the right-hand track downhill.

The next section takes you through a series of three more gates with about 200 metres between each one. About 80 metres after the third gate there is a split in the track. Take the right-hand path as it goes downhill to another gate 100 metres ahead. Pass through the gate and follow what can be a very muddy path for 700 metres through the woods to another gate. Go though the gate and towards the farm buildings ahead of you. Cross a stream over a bridge made from railway sleepers, then go through a gate and cross a ford (or footbridge if you wimp out). Turn right towards the farm buildings.

The house on your left just before you cross the railway line is Farworth Tea

Garden. If you fancy a drink and a piece of cake it's worth a stop here. If the tea garden is not obviously open, the owner suggests that you call at the house. If they are in, they will serve you with all manner of things. Check the opening times of the tea garden by phoning Mrs Eddon on 01751 477244.

After a stop at Farworth, cross the river and follow a wide forest track as it goes steeply uphill for half mile. At the top of the hill the track leaves the forest and levels out to a crossroads where you turn right. Pass houses on your right and continue along the level track for three-quarters of a mile where you come to a junction with East Brow house on your left.

Where the main track turns to the left around East Brow house, continue straight ahead on a wide track. After half a mile you come to a bridleway on your right which is the same one that you followed near the start of the route. Ignore this track and continue ahead for a further quarter of a mile to join a road. Turn left for the final 300 metres back to the start.

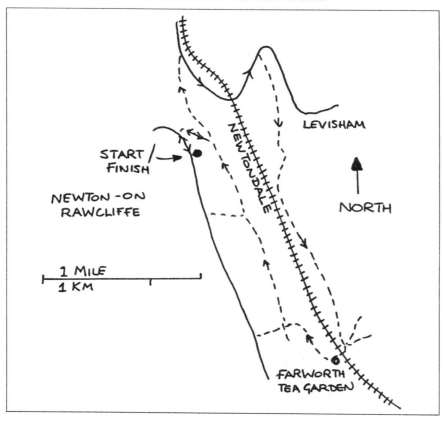

		LOCATION - NEWTONDALE	DISTANCE
80% OFFROAD		DIFFICULTY - MEDIUM WITH TWO STEEP HILLS	6.6 MILES
SPLIT DISTANCE	TOTAL DISTANCE	DESCRIPTION BETWEEN POINTS	DIAGRAM OF LOCATION
0	0	Start from the White swan public house in Newton-on-Rawcliff - Grid Ref. 813906 With your back to the pub, turn right and uphill	
0.11	0.11	Turn right onto a bridleway signed "Link Levisham 4 miles"	
0.29	0.4	Pass a footpath and then turn sharp left and downhill on a signed bridleway	
0.11	0.51	Ignore footpath on your right and continue ahead downhill through woods	
0.08	0.59	Through a gate and across a field with a hedge on your left	
0.16	0.75	Through gate and bear right downhill	
0.24	0.99	Through gate and them over a small river	
0.09	1.08	Turn right at a junction with a wide forest road	
0.46	1.54	Cross a railway line at Levisham station - Toilets and drinks machine are available on the station. There are band concerts & refreshments on Sundays in August	
0.02	1.56	Cross the cattle grid before a long steep uphill on tarmac	
0.63	2.19	Turn right onto a signed grassy bridleway keeping to the left of the gate	
0.2	2.39	Pass a footpath crossing the bridleway	

		LOCATION - NEWTONDALE	DISTANCE
80% OFFROAD		DIFFICULTY - MEDIUM WITH TWO STEEP HILLS	6.6 MILES
SPLIT DISTANCE	**TOTAL DISTANCE**	**DESCRIPTION BETWEEN POINTS**	**DIAGRAM OF LOCATION**
0.2	2.59	Ignore footpath on your left and continue on the main track towards Levisham Wood	
0.08	2.67	Through gate and turn right and downhill through the woods	
0.28	2.95	Through gate into open field with the railway on your right	
0.24	3.19	Through gate and keep right on track downhill	
0.11	3.3	Through gate	
0.06	3.36	Through gate	
0.14	3.5	Keep right and through gate	
0.09	3.59	Keep right and slightly downhill	
0.08	3.67	Through a gate and onto a track that can be very muddy during wet weather	
0.41	4.08	Out of the woods via a gate with the railway on your right	
0.17	4.25	Pass between two wire fences with farm buildings on your right	
0.04	4.29	Through a gate and cross the ford (or footbridge)	

SPLIT DISTANCE	TOTAL DISTANCE	LOCATION - NEWTONDALE DIFFICULTY - MEDIUM WITH TWO STEEP HILLS DESCRIPTION BETWEEN POINTS	DISTANCE 6.6 MILES DIAGRAM OF LOCATION
0.06	4.35	The house on your right before the railway crossing is Farworth tea garden - if it looks closed knock on the door & if you are lucky you will get a pot of tea and	
		cakes provided from Mrs Eddon. If you want to ring for opening times the number is 01751 477244 Continue over the railway and river then uphill	
0.1	4.45	Ignore a footpath on your right and continue uphill	
0.46	4.91	Turn right at crossroads towards houses on a signed bridleway	
0.76	5.67	Ignore a track on your right	
0.04	5.71	Ahead at junction with East Brow house on your left	
0.09	5.8	Ignore a track on your right	
0.25	6.05	Ignore a footpath on your left	
0.11	6.16	Ignore a bridleway on your left (the track you took earlier)	
0.3	6.46	Turn left onto tarmac and back to the car	
0.14	6.6	END	

Also from Sigma Leisure:

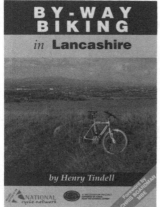

BY-WAY BIKING IN LANCASHIRE

Henry Tindell

From Morecambe Bay to Bolton and from Blackpool to Burnley, Henry Tindell reveals Lancashire's outstanding potential as a destination for mountain bikers.

"A fine variety of off-road tracks lead you to a wealth of countryside and villages all within easy reach of the large northern towns and cities". BOLTON ADVERTISER
£7.95

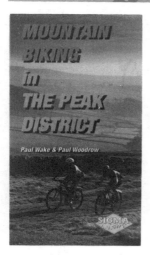

MOUNTAIN BIKING IN THE PEAK DISTRICT

Paul Wake and Paul Woodrow

18 varied routes, all within easy reach of the park's main tourist spots, which take in all that the area has to offer. Particular attention has been paid to the layout of the book - the routes are graded in terms of fitness and ability, and directions are clear and concise. "Although it is perfect for fairly serious mountain bikers - hence its inclusion of "lung busters" and a weekend-long ride - any mountain biker should be able to find routes in the book's pages to suit their limits." DERBYSHIRE TIMES
£7.95

All of our books are available through booksellers. In case of difficulty, or for a free catalogue, please contact: **SIGMA LEISURE, 1 SOUTH OAK LANE, WILMSLOW, CHESHIRE SK9 6AR.**
Phone: 01625-531035
Fax: 01625-536800.
E-mail: info@sigmapress.co.uk
Web site: http//www.sigmapress.co.uk
MASTERCARD and VISA orders welcome.